Guided Math

Made Easy

Grade 3

by Lisa Willman

Carson-Dellosa Publishing, LLC
Greensboro, North Carolina

Credits

Content Editors: Amy R. Gamble and Elizabeth Swenson

Copy Editor: Jesse Koziol

Layout Design: Van Harris

Cover Design: Lori Jackson

Visit *carsondellosa.com* for correlations to Common Core, state, national, and Canadian provincial standards.

Carson-Dellosa Publishing, LLC
PO Box 35665
Greensboro, NC 27425 USA
carsondellosa.com

ISBN 978-1-60996-470-2

04-123161151

Table of Contents

Skills Matrix..4

Introduction..5

Number and Operations

Identify place value to 10,000 6

Round numbers to the nearest ten, hundred, thousand 10

Add whole numbers with regrouping... 14

Subtract whole numbers across zeros 18

Use arrays to introduce concepts of multiplication 22

Multiplying multi-digit numbers by one-digit numbers 26

Divide whole numbers without remainders 30

Add simple fractions... 34

Algebra

Solve equations with variables.. 38

Solve equations with missing operation symbols 42

Solve word problems using equations.. 46

Geometric patterns 50

Analyze number patterns using tables....................................... 54

Measurement

Measure to the inch and the half inch....................................... 58

Calculate perimeter and area.. 62

Calculate volume of solid figures.. 66

Geometry

Identify and describe polygons 70

Identify and describe solids 74

Identify attributes of triangles.. 78

Data Analysis & Probability

Collect and represent data in a line plot 82

Collect and represent data in a bar graph 86

Conduct probability experiments and represent data 90

Answer Key 94

Skills Matrix

Page Numbers	Addition	Subtraction	Multiplication	Division	Place Value	Fractions	Patterns	Number Relationships	Measurement	Geometry	Data Analysis & Probability	Problem Solving
6–9					●			●				
10–13					●			●				
14–17	●				●							
18–21		●			●							
22–25	●		●									
26–29			●					●				
30–33				●				●				
34–37	●					●						
38–41	●	●	●	●				●				●
42–45	●	●	●	●				●				●
46–49	●	●	●	●				●				●
50–53							●			●		●
54–57							●	●				●
58–61									●			
62–65	●		●						●	●		
66–69			●						●	●		
70–73										●		
74–77										●		
78–81										●		
82–85											●	
86–89											●	
90–93						●					●	

CD-104563 © Carson-Dellosa

Introduction

One of the most challenging aspects of teaching mathematics is differentiating instruction to meet the needs of all of the learners in your classroom. As a classroom teacher, you are responsible for teaching the state and district standards that must be met by the end of the school year. But, the reality inside the classroom is that for some students the material is too difficult, while for others the material is too easy.

In the reading classroom, many teachers have found guided reading groups to be an excellent way to teach to the various levels of readers. In a small group setting, teachers are able to monitor the progress of students and vary instruction according to need.

This book provides a resource for using the same approach in the math classroom. The lessons are intended to supplement your existing curriculum. Throughout the year, refer to the lessons and activity sheets in *Guided Math Made Easy* to introduce topics, provide additional practice, or expand on learning.

Guided Math Made Easy is organized by the five National Council of Teachers of Mathematics (NCTM) content strands: Number and Operations, Algebra, Measurement, Geometry, and Data Analysis & Probability. Specific objectives were chosen from each strand to cover the areas with which third graders usually have the most difficulty or need additional classroom support.

For each objective, there is a teacher resource page. On these pages, mini-lessons are presented first. Mini-lessons are intended as your whole-group instruction to introduce each concept. Next, there are three group lessons. Group 1 is for below-level learners, Group 2 is for on-level learners, and Group 3 is for above-level learners. These hands-on group lessons can be used after the mini-lesson to practice or reinforce the skill. For below-level learners, group lessons can be used as pre-teaching lessons to introduce each topic.

After each teacher's page, three activity sheets are provided—one for each level of learner. These sheets can be used for review, sent home for homework, placed at a center, or used for informal assessments.

Key

Below Level:

On Level:

Above Level:

Number and Operations

Objective
Students will identify place value to 10,000.

Materials
- Index cards
- Tape
- Number cards 0–9
- Base ten blocks
- Activity sheets (pages 7–9)

Mini-Lesson

1. Write *ones*, *tens*, *hundreds*, *thousands*, and *ten thousands* on index cards. Tape the cards onto the board. Explain that the place value names help us talk about the digits and know their values.
2. Write *12,389* under the index cards.
3. Ask, "What is the place value of the digit 8? What is its value? Is it worth only 8?" Explain, "It means that there are 8 tens. Its value is 80." Demonstrate counting by 10 eight times until you get to 80.
4. Now, cover everything except the digits 8 and 9. Ask, "What if I needed to make up an addition problem to equal 89? What would the problem look like?" Write *80 + 9* on the board. Extend to the hundreds place. "The value of 3 hundreds is 300."
5. Continue working with other numbers, focusing on the place value names and their values.

Group 1 ○

Using Manipulatives to Identify Place Value

1. Give each student index cards with the place value names written on them (ones, tens, hundreds, thousands). Also, have number cards and base ten blocks available.
2. Have students put the index cards in the correct order in front of them. Using number cards, have them show you 1,267. Now, have them place the correct number of base ten blocks under each digit. Ask, "What digit is in the hundreds place? Which place is the 1 in?"
3. To determine the value of each number, count base ten blocks with the group. Ask, "How much does the 2 stand for? How much does the 6 stand for?"
4. Have students help you write the number in expanded form on the board. Explain as you go, "There is 1 thousand, so the value is 1,000. There are 2 hundreds, so the value is 200. Six tens is 60, and 7 ones is 7."

Group 2 ☐

Expanded Form to 10,000

1. Give each student a set of number cards, as well as index cards with the place value names written on them (ones, tens, hundreds, thousands).
2. Have students show you the number 9,823 by arranging the number cards under the place value cards.
3. Ask, "What digit is in the thousands place? What is the value of the 2? What is the place name of the 8?" Have students replace all of the number cards after the named digit with zeros to see its value.
4. Now, write the problem *50 + 2,000 + 7* on the board. Ask students to write the number in standard form. Ask, "What did you do when you noticed the numbers were not in descending order? How did you deal with the missing hundreds place value?"
5. Continue working with other numbers. Eventually, remove the index cards and have students work without them.

Group 3 △

Working with Numbers to 100,000

1. Give students a set of number cards and have them each choose five cards at random.
2. Have students make the smallest and then the largest number possible with the digits. Ask, "How did you make your decision to place the digits? How did you deal with zeros?"
3. Write *45,678* on the board. Have students write the number in expanded form. Ask, "If I added 5 ten thousands to this number, what would be the sum? What if I added 10 hundreds?" Have students use mental math and their knowledge of place value to solve the problems.
4. Write *45* on the board. Ask, "What is the answer if I multiply 10 times 45? What about 100 times 45 or 1,000 times 45?" Discuss how knowing place value is helpful for solving problems.
5. Continue adding, subtracting, and multiplying with other numbers, using place value as a guide.

Name_____

Write the place and the value of each underlined digit.

Number	Place	Value
3_4_5	___tens___	___40___
1. 2,1_3_4	_____	_____
2. 8_7_	_____	_____
3. _7_63	_____	_____
4. _6_,004	_____	_____
5. 9,_5_33	_____	_____
6. _4_87	_____	_____
7. 8,_2_09	_____	_____
8. 7_4_7	_____	_____
9. 9_1_	_____	_____
10. _8_,235	_____	_____

Write the expanded form of each number.
Example: $345 = 300 + 40 + 5$

11. 971 _____

12. 2,145 _____

13. 86 _____

14. 6,230 _____

15. 952 _____

Write the standard form of each expanded number.
Example: $300 + 40 + 5 = 345$

16. $700 + 40 + 3$ _____

17. $500 + 10 + 2$ _____

18. $80 + 6$ _____

19. $1,000 + 400 + 30$ _____

20. $3,000 + 600 + 30 + 7$ _____

Name_____

Write the place and the value of each underlined digit.

Number	Place	Value
1. <u>5</u>,879	_____	_____
2. 8,<u>1</u>23	_____	_____
3. 7,00<u>4</u>	_____	_____
4. <u>2</u>,589	_____	_____
5. 4,<u>2</u>34	_____	_____
6. 6,9<u>8</u>7	_____	_____
7. 4,7<u>1</u>7	_____	_____
8. 5,02<u>8</u>	_____	_____
9. <u>2</u>,369	_____	_____
10. 4,0<u>0</u>9	_____	_____

Write the expanded form of each number.

11. 5,897 _____

12. 2,308 _____

13. 5,230 _____

14. 7,876 _____

15. 3,876 _____

Write the standard form of each expanded number.

16. 3,000 + 400 + 50 + 8 _____

17. 4,000 + 600 + 80 + 1 _____

18. 3,000 + 500 + 20 + 3 _____

19. 60 + 4 + 2,000 + 500 _____

20. 700 + 30 + 4,000 + 5 _____

Name_____

Write the place and the value of each underlined digit.

Number	Place	Value
1. 28,9<u>0</u>8	_____	_____
2. 57,<u>1</u>45	_____	_____
3. 32,82<u>4</u>	_____	_____
4. <u>9</u>,008	_____	_____
5. <u>9</u>8,876	_____	_____

Write the expanded form of each number.

6. 38,812 _____

7. 32,687 _____

8. 59,004 _____

9. 38,912 _____

10. 40,045 _____

Write the standard form of each expanded number.

11. 30,000 + 4,000 + 700 + 50 + 3 _____

12. 60,000 + 3,000 + 400 + 70 + 1 _____

13. 4 + 200 + 5,000 + 30,000 + 80 _____

14. 50,000 + 20 + 7 _____

15. 7,000 + 4 + 70 + 200 + 60,000 _____

Solve each equation.

16. 45,345 + 10,000 _____

17. 67,432 + 30,000 _____

18. 94 × 10 _____

19. 67 × 1,000 _____

20. 854 × 100 _____

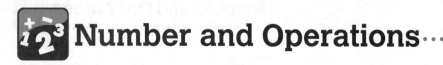

Number and Operations

Materials
- Self-stick notes
- Math notebooks
- Activity sheets (pages 11–13)

Objective
Round numbers to the nearest ten, hundred, thousand.

Mini-Lesson

1. Draw an illustration on the board of a hill with a car at the bottom left of the hill. Write the digits 1 to 9 along the hill so that 4 is slightly to the left of the top and 5 is slightly to the right of the top. Explain, "This is a very large hill and a very weak car; it takes large numbers for the car to get over the hill."
2. Write *26* on a self-stick note and place it on the car. Ask, "What 10 comes before 26? What is the next 10?" Write *20* and *30* on self-stick notes and place them on either side of the hill.
3. Say, "This hill can help us figure out how to round 26 to the nearest 10. If the number in the ones place is 5 or greater, we round to the greater 10." Demonstrate how the car makes it to 5 and rolls to the greater 10. "If the number in the ones column is 4 or less, we round down to the lesser 10." Show the car going up to 4 and rolling back down the hill.
4. Continue practicing with other numbers.

Group 1 ○

Rounding to Tens and Hundreds

1. Ask students to draw the hill and the car in their math notebooks. Have them label the hill with the digits 1 to 9.
2. Give each student a self-stick note with *52* written on it. Have students place the notes on the cars drawn in their notebooks. "How do we figure out what two 10s this number is between?" Point to the digit in the tens place and ask how this number gives a clue to the lesser 10. Then, have students find what 10 comes next by counting by tens. Have students write both tens on notes and place them on either side of the hill.
3. Have students move their 52 notes to the number along the hill that matches the number in the ones place. Have students move their 52 notes down the hill to the lesser 10. Ask students to explain when to round down to the lesser 10 and when to round up to the greater 10. Discuss how the number in the ones place lets us know whether to round up or down.

Group 2 □

Rounding to Hundreds and Thousands

1. Ask students to draw number lines in their math notebooks.
2. Write *376* on the board. Ask, "How do we figure out what two 100s this number is between?" Point to the digit in the hundreds place and ask how this number gives a clue to the lesser hundred. Then, ask students what hundred comes next. Write *300* and *400* on either side of the number line. Next, have students label the 10s on the number line (10 through 90).
3. Ask students to explain when to round down to the lesser 100 and when to round up to the greater 100. Have them draw a slash through the number line to show the point that separates the 10s that will round down and the 10s that will round up. Discuss how the number in the tens place lets us know whether to round up or down.
4. Practice rounding with 3-digit and 4-digit numbers, using the number line as a guide.

Group 3 △

Rounding to a Specific Place Value

1. Write the number *12,367* on the board. Underline the 2 in the thousands place.
2. Explain that sometimes we need to round to a specific place value, not just the digit with the greatest place value.
3. Ask students to explain their strategies for rounding to the number in the thousands place if a number is in the ten thousands place. Say, "This number is between 12,000 and 13,000. Which one is it closer to? Which digit will help me figure out if I should round up or down? What happens to the numbers in the hundreds, tens, and ones places?"
4. Continue practicing with other large numbers up to 6-digit numbers.

Name_____

Write the numbers 1 to 9 on the lines. Start at the car. Use the hill to help you solve the problems below.

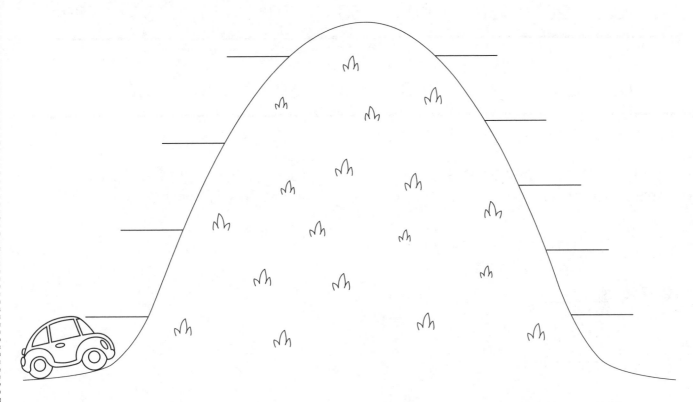

Round each number to the nearest ten.

1. 21 _____

2. 76 _____

3. 43 _____

4. 11 _____

5. 39 _____

6. 88 _____

7. 52 _____

8. 35 _____

9. 97 _____

10. 64 _____

Round each number to the nearest hundred.

11. 220 _____

12. 863 _____

13. 804 _____

14. 577 _____

15. 129 _____

16. 651 _____

17. 333 _____

18. 791 _____

19. 630 _____

20. 879 _____

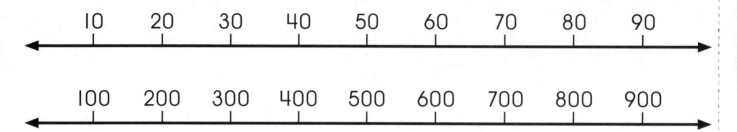
Name_____

Use the number lines to help you solve the problems below.

10   20   30   40   50   60   70   80   90

100   200   300   400   500   600   700   800   900

Round each number to the
nearest hundred.

1. 235 _____

2. 756 _____

3. 891 _____

4. 211 _____

5. 172 _____

6. 649 _____

7. 372 _____

8. 501 _____

9. 391 _____

10. 428 _____

Round each number to the
nearest thousand.

11. 1,872 _____

12. 9,124 _____

13. 4,871 _____

14. 6,199 _____

15. 8,293 _____

16. 2,009 _____

17. 5,877 _____

18. 3,500 _____

19. 7,220 _____

20. 9,701 _____

12

Name_____

Round each number to the underlined place value. Then, write the underlined digit's place value name.

	Rounded Number	Place Value of Underlined Digit
1. 2<u>1</u>	_____	_____
2. 14,8<u>7</u>4	_____	_____
3. <u>8</u>,378	_____	_____
4. <u>3</u>24	_____	_____
5. <u>6</u>8,011	_____	_____
6. 73,9<u>8</u>1	_____	_____
7. <u>8</u>7	_____	_____
8. <u>4</u>0,010	_____	_____
9. <u>5</u>50	_____	_____
10. 4,6<u>1</u>5	_____	_____
11. <u>6</u>8	_____	_____
12. <u>4</u>51	_____	_____
13. 1<u>0</u>,009	_____	_____
14. 6<u>0</u>2	_____	_____
15. <u>7</u>,234	_____	_____
16. 8<u>1</u>,513	_____	_____
17. <u>4</u>1	_____	_____
18. 2,<u>9</u>92	_____	_____
19. <u>5</u>2,876	_____	_____
20. 7<u>1</u>6	_____	_____

Number and Operations

Objective
Add whole numbers with regrouping.

Materials
- Base ten blocks
- Math notebooks
- Activity sheets (pages 15–17)

Mini-Lesson

1. Draw a chart on the board with columns for the ones and the tens. Write *29 + 45* vertically in the chart. Explain, "When we add, it is important to line up digits correctly—ones with ones and tens with tens."
2. "When I add 9 + 5, it equals 14, but there is only room for 1 digit." Demonstrate the concept of carrying with the base ten blocks. Put 9 cubes and 5 cubes together. Then, count the total (14). Say, "I trade 10 cubes for a tens rod and still have 14." Count blocks to confirm. "I write the 4 in the ones column because there are 4 cubes. Then, I carry the tens rod over to the tens column."
3. Point to the tens column. "I have 2 tens, 4 tens, and 1 ten for a total of 7 tens." Write *7* in the correct place.
4. Continue with other equations that require carrying.

Group 1 ○

Hands-On Adding
1. Have students draw ones and tens columns in their math notebooks.
2. Write *39 + 44* on the board to show students how to line up the problem by ones and tens. As you place base ten blocks, say, "The first number is 39, which has 3 tens and 9 ones; the second number has 4 tens and 4 ones." Have students count cubes along with you.
3. Say, "First, I add the ones column, 9 + 4." Pull all of the cubes together and count them. "Because I can't put the number 13 in the ones column, I trade 10 cubes for a tens rod. Now, I have 3 cubes left and 1 tens rod. I write *3* in the ones column. Then, I carry the tens rod to the tens column."
4. As you add the tens, explain, "3 tens + 4 tens + 1 ten = 8 tens." Have students count their own blocks with you and write the results in the appropriate columns. Ask students to read their sums. Read the entire equation, pointing to each addend and the sum on the board.
5. Continue practicing with equations that require regrouping.

Group 2 ☐

Carrying More Than Once
1. Write *3,644 + 2,839* on the board. Do the problem in front of the group, asking students to talk you through it as you work. Ask, "What column do I add first? Four + 9 equals 13. Can I put a 2-digit number in the ones column? Which digit do I write in the ones column and which in the tens column?"
2. Continue, "In the tens place, I add 4 tens + 3 tens + 1 ten. That equals 8 tens. Where do I write the 8? In the hundreds column, I add 6 hundreds + 8 hundreds, which equals 14 hundreds." Question students to have them help you regroup again.
3. Finish with the thousands column.
4. Continue with other numbers that require more than one regrouping. Ask students to try the problems on their own and check their work together.

Group 3 △

Is This Right?
1. Write *3,239 + 6,493 = 9,722* on the board. Tell students that you need their help. You know the problem is wrong. But, you don't know where the mistake is. Have students work the problem in their math notebooks and identify the mistake.
2. Discuss students' findings. "In the ones column, 9 + 3 = 12. The 2 was placed correctly in the ones column, but the ten was not carried to the tens column."
3. Continue with similar problems, such as *1,424 + 6,976 = 8,300*. Or, have students create problems for the group to solve.

Name_____

Solve each problem. Show your work.

1. $\begin{array}{r} 2\,3 \\ +\,6\,7 \\ \hline \end{array}$

2. $\begin{array}{r} 7\,6 \\ +\;\;5 \\ \hline \end{array}$

3. $\begin{array}{r} 5\,7 \\ +\,1\,6 \\ \hline \end{array}$

4. $\begin{array}{r} 2\,5 \\ +\,3\,5 \\ \hline \end{array}$

5. $\begin{array}{r} 6\,4 \\ +\,1\,8 \\ \hline \end{array}$

6. $\begin{array}{r} 4\,8 \\ +\,2\,2 \\ \hline \end{array}$

7. $\begin{array}{r} 4\,5 \\ +\,3\,0 \\ \hline \end{array}$

8. $\begin{array}{r} 1\,9 \\ +\,5\,8 \\ \hline \end{array}$

9. $\begin{array}{r} 1\,4 \\ +\,4\,3 \\ \hline \end{array}$

10. $\begin{array}{r} 7\,9 \\ +\;\;4 \\ \hline \end{array}$

11. $\begin{array}{r} 2\,9 \\ +\,4\,5 \\ \hline \end{array}$

12. $\begin{array}{r} 1\,3 \\ +\,6\,7 \\ \hline \end{array}$

13. $\begin{array}{r} 1\,6 \\ +\,7\,9 \\ \hline \end{array}$

14. $\begin{array}{r} 9\,8 \\ +\;\;1 \\ \hline \end{array}$

15. $\begin{array}{r} 7\,3 \\ +\,1\,7 \\ \hline \end{array}$

16. $\begin{array}{r} 7\,5 \\ +\,1\,0 \\ \hline \end{array}$

17. $\begin{array}{r} 2\,8 \\ +\,1\,9 \\ \hline \end{array}$

18. $\begin{array}{r} 6\,4 \\ +\,1\,7 \\ \hline \end{array}$

19. $\begin{array}{r} 3\,8 \\ +\,2\,9 \\ \hline \end{array}$

20. $\begin{array}{r} 2\,1 \\ +\,1\,9 \\ \hline \end{array}$

Name_____

Solve each problem. Show your work.

1. $\begin{array}{r} 362 \\ + 199 \\ \hline \end{array}$

2. $\begin{array}{r} 414 \\ + 397 \\ \hline \end{array}$

3. $\begin{array}{r} 298 \\ + 655 \\ \hline \end{array}$

4. $\begin{array}{r} 515 \\ + 225 \\ \hline \end{array}$

5. $\begin{array}{r} 198 \\ + 44 \\ \hline \end{array}$

6. $\begin{array}{r} 609 \\ + 91 \\ \hline \end{array}$

7. $\begin{array}{r} 724 \\ + 91 \\ \hline \end{array}$

8. $\begin{array}{r} 111 \\ + 457 \\ \hline \end{array}$

9. $\begin{array}{r} 672 \\ + 148 \\ \hline \end{array}$

10. $\begin{array}{r} 348 \\ + 484 \\ \hline \end{array}$

11. $\begin{array}{r} 3,459 \\ + 1,923 \\ \hline \end{array}$

12. $\begin{array}{r} 6,410 \\ + 3,190 \\ \hline \end{array}$

13. $\begin{array}{r} 8,009 \\ + 1,498 \\ \hline \end{array}$

14. $\begin{array}{r} 4,852 \\ + 4,167 \\ \hline \end{array}$

15. $\begin{array}{r} 2,066 \\ + 4,444 \\ \hline \end{array}$

16. $\begin{array}{r} 1,748 \\ + 3,471 \\ \hline \end{array}$

17. $\begin{array}{r} 5,617 \\ + 2,527 \\ \hline \end{array}$

18. $\begin{array}{r} 9,411 \\ + 254 \\ \hline \end{array}$

19. $\begin{array}{r} 6,240 \\ + 1,789 \\ \hline \end{array}$

20. $\begin{array}{r} 7,019 \\ + 1,942 \\ \hline \end{array}$

Name_____

Check the problems below. If the problem is correct, draw a star next to the problem. If the problem is incorrect, write the correct answer and a sentence explaining the mistake.

1.　　6,175　_____
　　+ 1,268　_____
　　　7,333　_____

2.　　9,481　_____
　　+ 292　_____
　　　9,673　_____

3.　　1,542　_____
　　+ 4,810　_____
　　　6,352　_____

4.　　81,276　_____
　　+ 19,484　_____
　　　90,750　_____

5.　　47,528　_____
　　+ 13,561　_____
　　　60,089　_____

6.　　20,451　_____
　　+ 70,769　_____
　　　91,220　_____

7.　　48,152　_____
　　+ 1,940　_____
　　　49,092　_____

8.　　64,591　_____
　　+ 31,655　_____
　　　95,146　_____

9.　　7,900　_____
　　+ 4,150　_____
　　　12,050　_____

10.　　52,578　_____
　　+ 9,412　_____
　　　51,980　_____

Number and Operations

Materials
- Base ten blocks
- Math notebooks
- Colored pencils
- Activity sheets (pages 19–21)

Objective
Subtract whole numbers across zeros.

Mini-Lesson

1. Write *80 – 25* on the board. Show the class 8 tens rods.
2. Say, "I want to take away 25 from this 80. I can take 20 (2 tens), but right now there aren't any ones to subtract the 5. So, I have to ungroup or borrow 1 of the tens from 80." Demonstrate trading a tens rod from the group of 8 tens for 10 cubes. Count the rods and the cubes to confirm that they still total 80.
3. Show the process on the equation. Say, "I'm going to cross off the 8 and write a 7 above it because I ungrouped one of the tens. Then, I cross off the 0 and write a 10 above it because I now have 10 ones."
4. Take away 5 ones and 2 tens. Ask students to help count how many are left. Record the answer and read the complete equation.
5. Have students work independently on the problem *61 – 34*. Observe any mistakes that students make. Teach to those mistakes and correct the problems together.

Group 1 ◯

Hands-On Subtracting

1. Provide students with base ten blocks.
2. Write *50 – 14* on the board. Say, "We start the problem with 50 blocks—5 tens and 0 ones." Count 5 tens rods with students.
3. Say, "Then, it says to take away 14. How many tens and ones are in 14? Can you take away the tens? The ones? Because I can't break these rods, I have to ungroup 1 of the tens." Take 1 tens rod and trade it for 10 cubes. After the trade, count all of the rods and cubes to show that they still total 50.
4. Demonstrate the process on the equation. "I ungrouped 1 of the tens. That left me with 4 tens." Cross off the 5 and write *4* above it. "I started with 0 ones and now I have 10." Cross off the 0 and write *10* above it. Take away 4 ones and 1 ten and record the solution.
5. Continue with other equations that require ungrouping.

Group 2 ▢

Using Drawings to Solve

1. Write *400 – 87* on the board. Draw 4 squares to represent 4 hundreds. Have students copy the problem and picture into their math notebooks.
2. Say, "Start with 400. We need to subtract 7 ones and 8 tens. Because we don't have any ones, go to the tens. Are there any tens? Where do we go next? Because there are no tens, ungroup one of the hundreds into 10 tens." With students, cross off one of the square blocks and draw 10 lines to represent tens rods. Show on the equation that there are 3 hundreds and 10 tens.
3. Say, "Now, ungroup 1 of the tens into 10 ones." In your drawing, represent the cubes with dots. Show in the problem that there are now 9 tens and 10 ones. Count to confirm that the total is still 400.
4. Have students use colored pencils to draw 8 tens and 7 ones in their notebooks. Write the results on the equation. Read the complete equation.
5. Continue with other equations that require multiple ungroupings.

Group 3 △

Using Estimating to Mentally Subtract

1. Write *3,000 – 1,345* on the board. Have students estimate the answer. Ask, "What did you round 1,345 to in order to estimate? How does rounding to the nearest hundred make it easier to mentally subtract?"
2. Now, ask students to find the exact answer. Compare their estimates to the exact answer. Ask, "How do they compare? What happens if we estimate to the nearest ten? Does that make it easier or more difficult to mentally calculate the answer?"
3. Demonstrate using estimating to find the exact answer to the problem above. Say, "I know I need 655 to round 1,345 to 2,000 (1,345 + 655 = 2,000). Then, I need 1,000 to get from 2,000 to 3,000 (2,000 + 1,000 = 3,000). Adding these numbers gives me the answer of 1,655 (1,000 + 655 = 1,655)."
4. Continue with other equations, having students explain their estimating thought processes.

Name_____

Solve each problem. Show your work.

1. $\begin{array}{r} 4\,0 \\ -\,1\,4 \end{array}$

2. $\begin{array}{r} 2\,0 \\ -\quad 9 \end{array}$

3. $\begin{array}{r} 9\,0 \\ -\,2\,5 \end{array}$

4. $\begin{array}{r} 7\,0 \\ -\,6\,2 \end{array}$

5. $\begin{array}{r} 3\,0 \\ -\,2\,2 \end{array}$

6. $\begin{array}{r} 5\,0 \\ -\,3\,3 \end{array}$

7. $\begin{array}{r} 8\,0 \\ -\,6\,9 \end{array}$

8. $\begin{array}{r} 7\,0 \\ -\,1\,5 \end{array}$

9. $\begin{array}{r} 6\,0 \\ -\,4\,1 \end{array}$

10. $\begin{array}{r} 2\,0 \\ -\,1\,6 \end{array}$

11. $\begin{array}{r} 9\,0 \\ -\,5\,7 \end{array}$

12. $\begin{array}{r} 4\,0 \\ -\,2\,8 \end{array}$

13. $\begin{array}{r} 5\,0 \\ -\,3\,6 \end{array}$

14. $\begin{array}{r} 8\,0 \\ -\,7\,7 \end{array}$

15. $\begin{array}{r} 6\,0 \\ -\,1\,4 \end{array}$

16. $\begin{array}{r} 3\,0 \\ -\,1\,8 \end{array}$

17. $\begin{array}{r} 5\,0 \\ -\,3\,9 \end{array}$

18. $\begin{array}{r} 4\,0 \\ -\,1\,0 \end{array}$

19. $\begin{array}{r} 6\,0 \\ -\,1\,4 \end{array}$

20. $\begin{array}{r} 8\,0 \\ -\,4\,2 \end{array}$

Name_____

Solve each problem. Show your work.

1. $\begin{array}{r} 30 \\ -18 \\ \hline \end{array}$	2. $\begin{array}{r} 90 \\ -22 \\ \hline \end{array}$	3. $\begin{array}{r} 40 \\ -11 \\ \hline \end{array}$	4. $\begin{array}{r} 80 \\ -35 \\ \hline \end{array}$	5. $\begin{array}{r} 70 \\ -46 \\ \hline \end{array}$
6. $\begin{array}{r} 400 \\ -23 \\ \hline \end{array}$	7. $\begin{array}{r} 500 \\ -124 \\ \hline \end{array}$	8. $\begin{array}{r} 900 \\ -368 \\ \hline \end{array}$	9. $\begin{array}{r} 700 \\ -414 \\ \hline \end{array}$	10. $\begin{array}{r} 800 \\ -350 \\ \hline \end{array}$
11. $\begin{array}{r} 6,000 \\ -1,400 \\ \hline \end{array}$	12. $\begin{array}{r} 8,000 \\ -2,042 \\ \hline \end{array}$	13. $\begin{array}{r} 3,000 \\ -1,243 \\ \hline \end{array}$	14. $\begin{array}{r} 2,000 \\ -24 \\ \hline \end{array}$	15. $\begin{array}{r} 9,000 \\ -409 \\ \hline \end{array}$
16. $\begin{array}{r} 1,000 \\ -421 \\ \hline \end{array}$	17. $\begin{array}{r} 4,000 \\ -422 \\ \hline \end{array}$	18. $\begin{array}{r} 5,000 \\ -1,495 \\ \hline \end{array}$	19. $\begin{array}{r} 7,000 \\ -5,084 \\ \hline \end{array}$	20. $\begin{array}{r} 4,000 \\ -3,421 \\ \hline \end{array}$

Name_____

First, estimate each answer. Then, solve.

1. $\begin{array}{r} 400 \\ -196 \\ \hline \end{array}$ Estimate: _____ Actual: _____	2. $\begin{array}{r} 600 \\ -241 \\ \hline \end{array}$ Estimate: _____ Actual: _____	3. $\begin{array}{r} 800 \\ -95 \\ \hline \end{array}$ Estimate: _____ Actual: _____
4. $\begin{array}{r} 200 \\ -45 \\ \hline \end{array}$ Estimate: _____ Actual: _____	5. $\begin{array}{r} 6,000 \\ -3,228 \\ \hline \end{array}$ Estimate: _____ Actual: _____	6. $\begin{array}{r} 2,000 \\ -850 \\ \hline \end{array}$ Estimate: _____ Actual: _____
7. $\begin{array}{r} 3,000 \\ -2,040 \\ \hline \end{array}$ Estimate: _____ Actual: _____	8. $\begin{array}{r} 7,000 \\ -4,727 \\ \hline \end{array}$ Estimate: _____ Actual: _____	9. $\begin{array}{r} 20,000 \\ -854 \\ \hline \end{array}$ Estimate: _____ Actual: _____
10. $\begin{array}{r} 80,000 \\ -24,043 \\ \hline \end{array}$ Estimate: _____ Actual: _____	11. $\begin{array}{r} 60,000 \\ -34,216 \\ \hline \end{array}$ Estimate: _____ Actual: _____	12. $\begin{array}{r} 10,000 \\ -894 \\ \hline \end{array}$ Estimate: _____ Actual: _____
13. $\begin{array}{r} 50,000 \\ -43 \\ \hline \end{array}$ Estimate: _____ Actual: _____	14. $\begin{array}{r} 70,000 \\ -44,444 \\ \hline \end{array}$ Estimate: _____ Actual: _____	15. $\begin{array}{r} 60,000 \\ -9,423 \\ \hline \end{array}$ Estimate: _____ Actual: _____

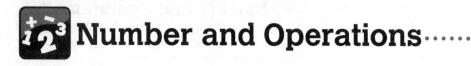

Number and Operations

Objective
Use arrays to introduce concepts of multiplication.

Materials
- Square tiles
- Chart paper
- Math notebooks
- Dice
- Graph paper
- Activity sheets (pages 23–25)

Mini-Lesson

1. Distribute square tiles to students and explain that you are working on an art project with tiles. Ask, "If the area is 5 tiles wide and 4 tiles long, how many tiles will I need in all?"
2. Allow time for students to explore with the tiles to develop an answer.
3. Model an array as a strategy to solve the problem. Say, "I need an area 4 tiles long and 5 tiles wide." (Place 4 tiles going down. Place 4 more tiles across beside the top tile.) "Now, I must fill in the space." (Fill the rectangular space with tiles.) "To find the answer, I can count each tile individually. Or, I can use repeated addition: 5 + 5 + 5 + 5 or 4 + 4 + 4 + 4 + 4." (Point to each row then column.) "I can also use multiplication: 5 x 4."
4. Draw the array on chart paper and label the sides. Write the addition and multiplication equations.
5. Continue working with other numbers. Have students record the arrays and equations in their math notebooks.

Group 1 ○

Creating Arrays
1. Have one student roll a pair of dice. Ask students to create square-tile arrays using the numbers rolled on the dice. One number tells how many tiles go across (columns), and the other number tells how many go down (rows).
2. Compare students' arrays. If a 3 and a 4 are rolled, ask, "Did anyone arrange the tiles 3 across and 4 down? What about 4 across and 3 down? Are these both correct?" Look for mistakes, such as adding an extra row by not counting the first in the column as one of the 4 down, resulting in 3 across and 5 down.
3. Discuss the addition problems that the arrays demonstrate: 3 + 3 + 3 + 3 or 4 + 4 + 4. Introduce multiplication: "Three rows of 4 tiles can be written as *3 x 4.*"
4. Have students record their arrays and equations on graph paper.
5. Continue with a new student rolling the dice.

Group 2 □

Using Arrays to Introduce Factor Pairs
1. Give each student 18 tiles. Ask students to create arrays using these tiles. Explain that all of the tiles must be used, and each array should create a rectangle. No tiles can be hanging off of the edge.
2. Have students record their arrays and the corresponding addition and multiplication problems on graph paper. Ask, "Can the same 18 tiles be arranged in a different way?" Challenge students to arrange the 18 tiles in all of the 3 possible ways.
3. Record all of the different arrays that students created on chart paper: 1 x 18, 2 x 9, 3 x 6. Introduce the new vocabulary words *factor* and *factor pairs.* List the factor pairs of 18.
4. Continue giving students new numbers to find factor pairs for. Have students record their results in their math notebooks.

Group 3 △

Using Arrays to Develop Vocabulary
1. Ask students to draw all of the arrays for the number 24 on graph paper.
2. As a group, list all of the multiplication equations for 24. Introduce the vocabulary words *factor* and *factor pairs* during the discussion. Ask, "What are the factors for 24? What are the factor pairs for 24?"
3. Next, ask students to find all of the arrays for the number 11. When students determine that this number has only one possible array, introduce the vocabulary words *prime* and *composite.* "What do the words *prime* and *composite* mean? How do these words relate to the numbers 24 and 11?"
4. Now, ask students to draw the 3 x 3 array for the number 9. Ask students to study the array. "What shape is this array? What do you notice about this factor pair?" Introduce the vocabulary term *square numbers.* "What is this type of number called?"
5. Continue working with other numbers while reinforcing the vocabulary.

Name_____

Solve each problem. Show your work.

Step 1: Roll two dice.

Step 2: Draw an array that uses both numbers.

Step 3: Write the repeated addition problem and the multiplication problem.

Example: I rolled a __3__ and a __4__ .

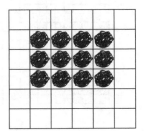

4 + 4 + 4 = 12

3 x 4 = 12

1. I rolled a ___ and a ___ .

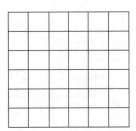

_____

_____

2. I rolled a ___ and a ___ .

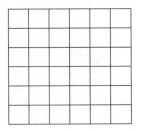

_____

_____

3. I rolled a ___ and a ___ .

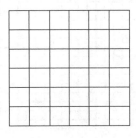

_____

_____

4. I rolled a ___ and a ___ .

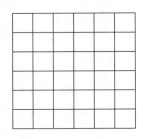

_____

_____

5. I rolled a ___ and a ___ .

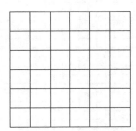

_____

_____

Name_____

Draw and label all of the arrays that can be made for each given number. Then, list all of the factors and factor pairs.

Example:
12

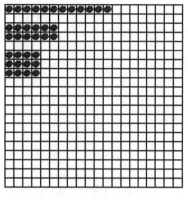

Factors: <u>1, 2, 3, 4, 6, 12</u>

Factor Pairs: <u>1, 12; 2, 6; 3, 4</u>

1.
10

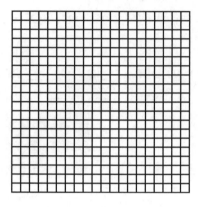

Factors: _____

Factor Pairs: _____

2.
13

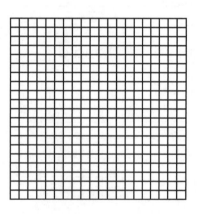

Factors: _____

Factor Pairs: _____

3.
15

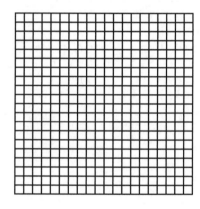

Factors: _____

Factor Pairs: _____

4.
16

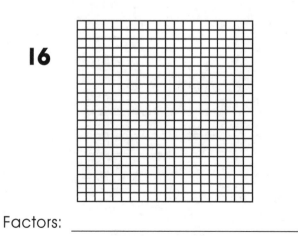

Factors: _____

Factor Pairs: _____

5.
18

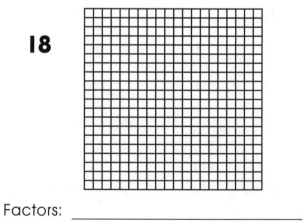

Factors: _____

Factor Pairs: _____

24

Name_____

Answer the following questions.

1. List ten prime numbers. _____

2. List ten square numbers. _____

3. List ten composite numbers. _____

4. What are the factor pairs of 30? _____

5. Draw and label the arrays for the number 20.

6. Draw and label the arrays for the number 36.

7. Draw and label the arrays for the number 48.

8. Draw and label the arrays for the number 50.

9. Explain the difference between prime numbers and composite numbers.

_____

_____

10. Explain factors and factor pairs. Use drawings to illustrate your answer.

_____

_____

Number and Operations

Materials
- Counters
- Math notebooks
- Activity sheets (pages 27–29)

Objective
Multiplying multi-digit numbers by one-digit numbers

Mini-Lesson

1. Write the problem *25 x 3* on the board. Ask, "How will I solve this problem if I don't know factors past 10?"
2. Model different strategies to solve the problem. Say, "When I saw the number 25, I immediately thought of quarters. I know that 3 quarters are equal to 75 cents. So, 25 x 3 equals 75. Because I'm only multiplying by 3, I also could do a repeated addition problem: 25 + 25 + 25. Another way to solve this is by doing problems I already know. For example, I can break down 25 into 20 + 5 and multiply both numbers by 3: 20 x 3 = 60 and 5 x 3 = 15. Then, I add 60 + 15, and that equals 75."
3. Continue practicing and encourage students to use their sense of numbers to solve additional multiplication problems.

Group 1 ◯

Using Counters to Multiply
1. Provide students with counters.
2. Write the problem *11 x 3* on the board. Say, "How can the counters help solve this problem?" Create 3 separate groups with 11 counters in each group. Show the addition problem *11 + 11 + 11* while pointing to the 3 groups. Explain that multiplication is a shorter way to represent repeated addition.
3. Now, write the problem *12 x 4*. Have students use the counters to solve the problem. Have students write the addition problems that they used to solve the problem in their math notebooks.
4. Continue working with multi-digit numbers under 20.

Group 2 ◻

Solving Multiple Ways
1. Write the problem *24 x 7* on the board. Ask students to use their own methods to solve the problem in their math notebooks. Have students share their ways to solve the problem.
2. First, write *24* seven times and add. Next, demonstrate how to round 24 up to 25. Then, mentally calculate that seven 25s equals 175. Then, subtract 7 because you rounded up 1 seven times.
3. Use the traditional method. Multiply the ones (4 x 7) and carry the 2 tens. Then, multiply 7 x 2 and add the 2 tens.
4. Ask, "How can 24 be written in terms of tens and ones?" Model as you split 24 into numbers that can easily be multiplied in students' heads. "Twenty-four is the same as 20 + 4. How will writing 24 like this make multiplying it by 7 easier?" Model multiplying both 20 and 4 by 7: 20 x 7 = 140 and 4 x 7 = 28. Ask, "What should I do with these products to find the final answer to 24 x 7?" Then, add 140 + 28 to equal 168.
5. Let students practice the various methods with additional problems.

Group 3 △

Working with Larger Numbers
1. Write the problem *251 x 6* on the board. Ask students to solve the problem independently.
2. Ask students to write 251 in expanded form with the addends stacked vertically and aligned by place value. Then, beside each number, have them write x 6 = and the resulting products. Show students how to find the sum of the expanded number (251), repeat x 6 =, and find the sum of the products (1506).

$$
\begin{array}{r}
200 \times 6 = 1200 \\
50 \times 6 = 300 \\
+ \ 1 \times 6 = 6 \\
\hline
251 \times 6 = 1506
\end{array}
$$

Discuss how the expanded form of a number can help you solve the problem.
3. Now, write *3,456 x 8* on the board. Have students use the expanded form strategy to solve the problem in their math notebooks. Then, discuss how they broke down 3,456 to solve the problem in the most efficient way.
4. Encourage students to compute additional problems using mental math strategies instead of writing them out.

Name_____

Write the repeated addition problem for each equation. Then, solve. Show your work with numbers or drawings.

1. $10 \times 2 =$

2. $15 \times 4 =$

3. $12 \times 2 =$

4. $14 \times 3 =$

5. $10 \times 6 =$

6. $11 \times 3 =$

7. $13 \times 4 =$

8. $16 \times 0 =$

9. $20 \times 4 =$

10. $12 \times 5 =$

11. $10 \times 5 =$

12. $13 \times 2 =$

13. $14 \times 1 =$

14. $11 \times 2 =$

15. $15 \times 3 =$

16. $18 \times 3 =$

Name_____

Solve each problem. Show your work. Demonstrate what method you used to solve.

1. 40 × 2 =   2. 24 × 5 =

3. 71 × 6 =   4. 88 × 5 =

5. 40 × 9 =   6. 110 × 3 =

7. 4 × 37 =   8. 68 × 2 =

9. 27 × 3 =   10. 18 × 6 =

11. 250 × 6 =   12. 33 × 3 =

13. 50 × 10 =   14. 200 × 7 =

15. 48 × 4 =   16. 45 × 4 =

CD-104563

Name_____

Solve each problem. Show your work with expanded numbers.

1. 384 × 6 =

2. 637 × 5 =

3. 521 × 3 =

4. 801 × 9 =

5. 467 × 8 =

6. 169 × 2 =

7. 525 × 8 =

8. 248 × 7 =

9. 714 × 4 =

10. 925 × 5 =

11. 1,245 × 3 =

12. 2,567 × 5 =

13. 8,205 × 8 =

14. 4,670 × 2 =

15. 5,254 × 6 =

16. 445 × 9 =

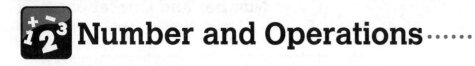

Number and Operations

Materials
- Counters
- Math notebooks
- Activity sheets (pages 31–33)

Objective
Divide whole numbers without remainders.

Mini-Lesson

1. Give each student 10 counters. Explain that there are 10 cookies and 5 friends. How can the cookies be divided so that each friend has the same amount?
2. Draw 5 stick people on the board and have students draw 5 people in their math notebooks. Give each stick person a counter as you say, "One for you, one for you," and so on. Have students use their counters to follow along. After each stick person has 1 counter, some counters are left. Ask, "What should I do with the rest of the counters?" Give each stick person a second counter. Then, point out that each stick person has 2 counters. There are no remainders.
3. Write the equation $10 \div 5 = 2$ on the board. Explain, "There were 10 cookies divided among 5 friends. Each of the 5 friends got 2 cookies. There are none left over. Ten divided by 5 equals 2."
4. Continue with other simple numbers that divide evenly.

Group 1 ◯

Making Equal Groups
1. Place counters within students' reach. Write the problem $12 \div 2$ on the board.
2. Point to the 12. "This number tells us how many to start with." Ask students to take 12 counters. Then, point to the 2. "This number tells how many groups to make." Have students draw 2 large circles in their math notebooks. Demonstrate how to place the counters one at a time, evenly between the 2 groups. "The answer, or the *quotient*, tells us how many are in each group. What is the quotient?" Read the complete equation together: 12 divided by 2 equals 6.
3. Ask, "What would happen if I had counters left over? Can I just make one group bigger? If I divided cookies between friends, would it be fair to give one person more than the others?" Explain that when you divide, each group must be equal.
4. Continue with numbers that can be evenly divided.

Group 2 ▢

Relationship between Division and Multiplication
1. Write $4 + 6 = 10$ and $10 - 6 = 4$ on the board. Discuss how addition and subtraction are inverse operations.
2. Now, write the problem $25 \div 5$ on the board. Ask, "How can this problem be solved with a relationship similar to that of addition and subtraction? What do we know about the relationship between multiplication and division?" Explain that multiplication and division are also inverse operations.
3. Write $5 \times \underline{\quad} = 25$ on the board. Ask, "What times 5 equals 25? Twenty-five divided into 5 groups has 5 in each group." Use the counters in an array to demonstrate 5 rows of 5 to confirm the solution.
4. Continue with other numbers, practicing using the relationship between multiplication and division.

Group 3 △

Input and Output
1. Draw a T-chart on the board. Write the following numbers on the left side of the line: *45, 60, 30, 15*. Write the following numbers on the right side of the line: *9, 12, 6, 3*.
2. Explain that this is an input/output chart. "When 45 is put in the chart, 9 comes out. When 60 is put in, 12 comes out. What rule is applied to 45 and 60?" Emphasize that the rule has to be true for every number.
3. Discuss the strategies that students used to figure out that the rule is "divide by 5."
4. Continue with a new chart. Write *36, 72, 45,* and *18* on the left and *4, 8, 5,* and *2* on the right. Work with charts that have one or more numbers missing. Have students figure out the rule and what is missing. For example, write *66, 24, 36,* and *___* on the left and write *11, ___, 6,* and *7* on the right.

Name_____

Solve each problem. Show your work with numbers or drawings.

1. $12 \div 4$

2. $9 \div 3$

3. $30 \div 5$

4. $15 \div 3$

5. $14 \div 7$

6. $13 \div 1$

7. $20 \div 5$

8. $18 \div 3$

9. $4 \div 4$

10. $8 \div 2$

11. $24 \div 6$

12. $21 \div 7$

13. $16 \div 4$

14. $6 \div 2$

15. $22 \div 11$

16. $27 \div 3$

Name_____

Solve each division problem. Then, complete the multiplication problem that relates to the division problem. Show your work with numbers or drawings.

1. 72 ÷ 8 = ____   8 × ____ = 72   2. 54 ÷ 9 = ____   9 × ____ = 54

3. 16 ÷ 4 = ____   4 × ____ = 16   4. 18 ÷ 2 = ____   2 × ____ = 18

5. 48 ÷ 6 = ____   6 × ____ = 48   6. 63 ÷ 7 = ____   7 × ____ = 63

7. 36 ÷ 9 = ____   9 × ____ = 36   8. 40 ÷ 10 = ____   10 × ____ = 40

9. 15 ÷ 3 = ____   3 × ____ = 15   10. 32 ÷ 8 = ____   8 × ____ = 32

11. 25 ÷ 5 = ____   5 × ____ = 25   12. 27 ÷ 3 = ____   3 × ____ = 27

13. 24 ÷ 4 = ____   4 × ____ = 24   14. 40 ÷ 8 = ____   8 × ____ = 40

15. 30 ÷ 5 = ____   5 × ____ = 30   16. 45 ÷ 5 = ____   5 × ____ = 45

CD-104563 © Carson-Dellosa

Name_____

Solve each problem. Show your work with expanded numbers. For numbers 7–8, create your own input/output charts.

1. The rule is: _____

90	9
30	3
70	7
40	4

2. The rule is: _____

45	9
60	12
30	___
___	4

3. The rule is: _____

120	6
80	4
160	___
___	5

4. The rule is: _____

24	___
15	5
___	9
12	4

5. The rule is: _____

90	6
30	___
105	7
___	5

6. The rule is: _____

77	11
84	___
168	24
___	9

7. The rule is: _____

8. The rule is: _____

Number and Operations

Objective
Add simple fractions.

Materials
- Counters
- Math notebooks
- Activity sheets (pages 35–37)

Mini-Lesson

1. Draw a rectangle on the board. Explain that it represents a submarine sandwich. The sandwich shop divided it into 4 equal sections. Draw 3 lines in the rectangle to divide it into 4 equal sections.
2. The first day, a boy ate 1 of the 4 pieces (1/4 of the sandwich). Shade 1 of the 4 rectangles. The next day, the boy was very hungry and ate 2 of the 4 pieces (2/4). Shade 2 of the rectangles with another color. Ask, "How much of the sandwich did the boy eat in total?"
3. Write ___ + ___ = ___ on the board. First, ask how many sections the sandwich is divided into. Write this number as the denominator of all of the fractions. Point out that when adding fractions, the denominator remains the same because the total number of pieces of the sandwich never changes.
4. Then, ask how many pieces of the sandwich were eaten each day. Write those numbers as the numerators of the first two fractions. Explain that it is the top number, or the numerator, that changes. Ask students to add the number of pieces eaten to complete the last fraction. Read the complete equation.
5. Continue with other fractions with like denominators.

Group 1 ◯

Adding Simple Fractions

1. Draw a rectangle on the board. Next to it, write the equation *1/3 + 1/3 = ___* . Have students draw the same rectangle in their math notebooks. Say, "The bottom number, the denominator, tells us how many parts to divide our rectangle into." Help students divide their rectangles into 3 equal parts. Explain, "The total number of parts will not change, so write *3* as the denominator of the answer."
2. Continue, "The first number, 1/3, means 1 of the 3 parts. So, I am going to shade one of the parts. The second number, 1/3, tells us to shade in 1 more part." Have students shade their rectangles. Say, "It's an addition problem, so I'm going to add these shaded sections together." Say, "One plus 1 equals 2," and write *2* as the numerator of the answer.
3. Point to the parts of the rectangle as you read the complete equation: "One-third of the rectangle plus another 1/3 equals 2/3 of the whole rectangle."
4. Continue with other equations with like denominators.

Group 2 ☐

Fractions of a Whole

1. Have students draw a rectangle in their math notebooks. Ask them to divide their rectangles into 8 equal sections. Ask, "What will the denominator be for fractions about this rectangle?"
2. Tell students to shade 3 sections of their rectangles. "What fraction of the rectangle did you shade? Write the fraction in your notebooks."
3. Ask, "How many more sections of the rectangle would you need to shade for the rectangle to be completely shaded? What fraction represents that number of sections? Write the fraction in your notebooks."
4. Say, "Now use the two fractions to write an addition problem. What is the sum? What is another way to write this sum?" Guide students to see the relationship between 8/8 and 1 whole rectangle.
5. Continue with other fractions.

Group 3 △

Improper Fractions and Mixed Numbers

1. Write *2/4 + 3/4* on the board. Next to it, draw a rectangle divided into 4 sections.
2. Shade 2 of the 4 sections. Say, "The second part of the equation tells me to add 3 sections, but I only have 2 sections left. What should I do?" Draw a new rectangle that is divided into 4 sections. "Now do I have 3 sections to shade?" Shade 1 section of the second rectangle.
3. Ask students to add the fractions and write the sum (5/4). Explain, "Because the numerator is larger than the denominator, this is called an improper fraction. We can convert an improper fraction into a mixed number, which includes a whole number and fraction." Show on the board how 1 whole rectangle was filled in along with 1 of the 4 pieces of the second. Ask students to write 5/4 as a mixed number (1 1/4).
4. Continue with other equations that produce improper fractions.

Name_____

Solve each problem. Show your work with drawings.

Example: $\frac{1}{6} + \frac{2}{6} = \frac{3}{6}$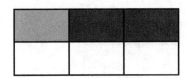

1. $\frac{1}{4} + \frac{1}{4}$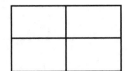

2. $\frac{1}{6} + \frac{3}{6}$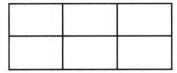

3. $\frac{5}{8} + \frac{2}{8}$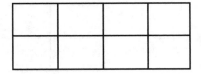

4. $\frac{1}{3} + \frac{1}{3}$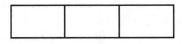

5. $\frac{1}{8} + \frac{4}{8}$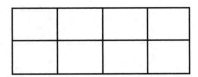

6. $\frac{2}{4} + \frac{1}{4}$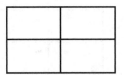

7. $\frac{2}{8} + \frac{4}{8}$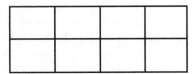

8. $\frac{1}{6} + \frac{2}{6}$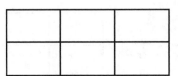

9. $\frac{1}{4} + \frac{1}{4} + \frac{1}{4}$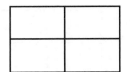

10. $\frac{1}{2} + \frac{1}{2}$

Name_____

Shade each rectangle to show the given fraction. Then, write an addition problem that equals 1 whole.

Example: $\frac{3}{6} + \frac{3}{6} = 1$

1. $\frac{1}{2}$

_____

2. $\frac{1}{3}$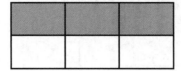

_____

3. $\frac{1}{5}$

_____

4. $\frac{1}{8}$

_____

5. $\frac{1}{6}$

_____

6. $\frac{2}{4}$

_____

7. $\frac{3}{8}$

_____

8. $\frac{2}{5}$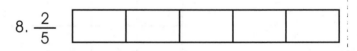

_____

9. $\frac{3}{10}$

_____

10. $\frac{2}{8}$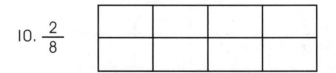

_____

Name_____

Solve each problem. Then, convert improper fractions to mixed numbers. Show your work with drawings.

Example: $\dfrac{5}{6} + \dfrac{2}{6} = \dfrac{7}{6} = 1\dfrac{1}{6}$

1. $\dfrac{1}{5} + \dfrac{5}{5} =$

2. $\dfrac{5}{6} + \dfrac{2}{6} =$

3. $\dfrac{2}{4} + \dfrac{3}{4} =$

4. $\dfrac{3}{4} + \dfrac{3}{4} =$

5. $\dfrac{2}{3} + \dfrac{2}{3} + \dfrac{1}{3} =$

6. $\dfrac{3}{6} + \dfrac{2}{6} + \dfrac{2}{6} =$

7. $\dfrac{4}{10} + \dfrac{7}{10} =$

8. $\dfrac{2}{4} + \dfrac{1}{4} + \dfrac{3}{4} =$

9. $\dfrac{3}{10} + \dfrac{4}{10} + \dfrac{8}{10} =$

10. $\dfrac{2}{5} + \dfrac{3}{5} + \dfrac{4}{5} =$

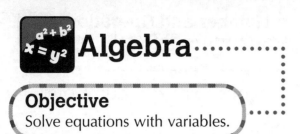

Algebra

Objective
Solve equations with variables.

Materials
- *Balancing Act* by Ellen Stoll Walsh (Beach Lane Books, 2010)
- Counters
- Paper
- Self-stick notes
- Activity sheets (pages 39–41)

Mini-Lesson

1. Read *Balancing Act* to the class. Balancing is a great metaphor to use while teaching algebra. Explain that an equation is like a teeter-totter. Both sides need to be equal for it to be balanced. If one side is greater, the equation is no longer equal. This type of equation uses a "not equal to" sign: $3 + 4 \neq 9$.
2. Traditionally, problems are written as $4 + 5 = 9$. But, they can also be written as $9 = 4 + 5$ or $2 + 7 = 4 + 5$, as long as both sides of the equation are balanced or equal.
3. Write the equation $10 = 5 + \underline{\quad}$. Ask, "What can I add to 5 to equal 10 and make this a balanced number sentence?"
4. Continue working with other number sentences with missing variables.

Group 1 ○

Working with Counters

1. Write the equation $7 + \underline{\quad} = 10$ on the board. Give each student 7 counters. "We start with 7. We need to add an unknown number to 7 so that it equals 10 counters. What are some ways to solve this?"
2. Discuss various strategies. Count aloud while modeling with the counters. "I start with 7 and continue counting: 8, 9, 10. I added 3 counters to get to 10."
3. Demonstrate how to work backward with the counters. Start with 10 counters. Explain that the counters need to be divided into two groups. "We know that there are 7 counters in one group. How many will be in the second group?"
4. Continue working with other number sentences with missing variables.

Group 2 ▢

Determining Missing Numbers

1. Write the number *100* on the board. Ask students to write an equation that equals 100 on each side of the equal sign. Write their answers on the board. Include a variety of examples of the equation. Some possibilities include $30 + 70 = 100$, $100 = 30 + 70$, $50 + 50 = 20 + 80$, $10 + 50 + 40 = 20 + 20 + 60$.
2. Now, choose one of the problems and cover one of its numbers with a self-stick note. Ask, "How can we calculate the missing number? Is there only one possibility for the number? What if a number were missing from each side of the equation?"
3. Have students write their own balanced equations on sheets of paper. Give each student a self-stick note to cover one number in her equation. Collect the papers and have the group work together to solve for each unknown number. Uncover the notes to check the answers.

Group 3 △

Solving for Variables

1. Write the number sentence $100 + 100 = n + 80$ on the board. Ask, "What total does each side of the equal sign need to make a balanced equation? What does the n stand for?"
2. Discuss various strategies to solve the problem. "What are some mental math strategies that can help solve this problem? What operation can be performed on the known numbers to find the value of the variable?"
3. Write five problems on the board: $1,500 + n = 2,000$; $210 = 45 + n$; $300 + 55 = 200 + n$; $12 + n = 150 + 20$; $100 - 20 = 10 + n$. Have students solve for n in each equation.
4. Ask students to write in their math notebooks about how they solved the problems. What were their thoughts? Many times, the above-level students "just know it." Work on verbalizing their solutions. What do they know about numbers that helped them solve each equation?

Name_____

Write the missing number in each equation.

1. $4 + \underline{\quad} = 11$

2. $15 = 10 + \underline{\quad}$

3. $2 + \underline{\quad} = 4 + 2$

4. $12 - \underline{\quad} = 8$

5. $\underline{\quad} = 6 + 6$

6. $1 + 8 = 4 + \underline{\quad} + 4$

7. $\underline{\quad} + 10 = 13$

8. $6 + 3 = 3 + \underline{\quad}$

9. $9 = \underline{\quad} + 1$

10. $18 - 9 = \underline{\quad}$

11. $10 = 5 + 1 + \underline{\quad}$

12. $\underline{\quad} - 6 = 3$

13. $3 + 4 + \underline{\quad} = 1 + 4 + 4$

14. $8 + 2 = \underline{\quad}$

15. $16 = \underline{\quad} + 4$

16. $13 + 2 = 15 + \underline{\quad}$

17. $6 + 6 + 2 = \underline{\quad}$

18. $\underline{\quad} + 7 = 7 + 3$

19. $2 + 3 + \underline{\quad} = 8$

20. $20 + \underline{\quad} = 2 + 20$

Name_____

Write the missing number in each equation.

1. 12 + ____ = 8 + 12

2. 24 = ____ + 15

3. 10 + 25 = ____ + 30

4. 30 – 5 = ____

5. 6 + 12 = 12 + ____

6. ____ = 20 + 25

7. 67 + ____ = 70

8. 100 + ____ = 142

9. 30 + 20 + 5 = ____ + 20 + 25

10. ____ + 15 = 15 + 5

11. ____ – 20 = 40

12. 40 + ____ = 60

13. ____ + 60 = 30 + 70

14. 50 = ____ + 25

15. ____ = 300 + 67

16. 100 = ____ + 30

17. ____ = 12 + 12 + 10

18. 80 – ____ = 30

19. 20 + 30 + 10 = 40 + ____ + 10

20. 40 + 23 = ____ + 60

40

Name_____

Solve for the variable in each equation.

1. $100 + 30 = 50 + n$

2. $20 + 30 + 100 = n$

3. $n = 300 + 400$

4. $45 + 20 = 20 + n$

5. $500 = 45 + n$

6. $800 + n = 930$

7. $580 + 20 = n$

8. $9,800 = 4,000 + n$

9. $60 + n = 12 + 60$

10. $3,000 + 3,000 + n = 8,000$

11. $n + 39 = 670 + 9$

12. $670 - n = 605$

13. $6000 = 5,800 + n$

14. $1,400 + 500 = n + 1,400$

15. $3,480 = 400 + 80 + n$

16. $458 = n + 50 + 200 + 200$

17. $4,000 + 3,000 + 7,000 = 10,000 + n$

18. $7,000 + n + 38 = 6,000 + 38 + 1,000$

19. $5,000 + 400 + 30 + 7 = 400 + n + 7 + 30$

20. $30 + 40 + 5,000 + 600 = 2,000 + n + 70 + 600$

 **Algebra**

Objective
Solve equations with missing operation symbols.

Materials
- *Equal Shmequal* by Virginia L. Kroll (Charlesbridge Publishing, 2005)
- Index cards
- Number cards
- Math notebooks
- Activity sheets (pages 43–45)

Mini-Lesson

1. Read *Equal Shmequal* to illustrate how an equation needs both sides of the equal sign to be balanced. It is an effective visual tool for the algebra strand.
2. Explain that all of the operation signs in the math book disappeared last night, so today students need to work as math detectives to look for clues to solve equations. Review the four operation signs and what they mean. Remind students that the operation sign used must make both sides of the equation equal.
3. Write *10 ____ 5 = 15* on the board. Say, "The left side of the equal sign has two lesser numbers, while the right side has a greater number. Which two operations result in an answer that is a greater number? If these numbers are multiplied, the product would be too big. But, if I add, 10 plus 5 equals 15." Write a plus sign in the box.
4. Continue with other number sentences.

Group 1 ○

Guess the Missing Symbol
1. Give each student three index cards and a deck of number cards. Have students write a different symbol (+, −, and =) on each index card.
2. Write *6 ____ 3 = 9* on the board. Have students place their cards on the table to match the equation. Instruct students to place the correct operation sign cards to make the equation true. Write a plus sign in the equation on the board. Ask, "Does this make sense? How did you know which operation sign to use? Would a subtraction sign be correct?" Observe students who easily understand the relationship between the numbers.
3. Continue with other number sentences, using a variety of ways to write each equation. Some possibilities include *3 + 4 = 7, 7 = 3 + 4,* and *1 + 6 = 3 + 4.*

Group 2 ▢

Creating Balanced Equations
1. Give each student five index cards and a deck of number cards. Have students write a different symbol (+, −, x, ÷, and =) on each index card.
2. Have students separate the number cards 4, 5, and 9. Ask, "How can we combine these cards with some of the index cards to make a true number sentence?" Give students time to manipulate their cards.
3. Ask, "How can we arrange the numbers so that the answer is greater (or less) than the numbers with the operation sign? Which operation uses this arrangement?" Arrange the cards as *4 + 5 = 9, 9 = 4 + 5, 9 − 5 = 4,* or *9 − 4 = 5.* All of these equations keep both sides of the equal sign balanced.
4. Ask students to create a new equation with their cards. Then, have them remove the symbols. Go around the table as students solve each other's equations. Discuss the clues they use to determine the signs.

Group 3 △

What Do You Do First?
1. Write *35 = (4 ____ 9) ____ 1.* Have students find the missing operation symbols.
2. Discuss the purpose of the parentheses. Explain that they let us know what to do first in the problem.
3. Discuss strategies to correctly place the missing signs. Are there other possible answers? As students work on these types of problems, they may find that sometimes many solutions are possible.
4. Have each student create a number sentence for the rest of the group. Then, have the group solve everyone's equation. While they work, observe the accuracy of the equations, the complexity of the problems, and the ease of solving them.

Name_____

Write the missing operation signs.

1. 4 ____ $9 = 13$

2. 3 ____ $7 = 10$

3. 4 ____ $5 = 20$

4. 15 ____ $5 = 10$

5. 8 ____ $2 = 6$

6. 2 ____ $6 = 12$

7. 10 ____ $5 = 2$

8. 6 ____ $5 = 30$

9. 20 ____ $10 = 10$

10. 25 ____ $5 = 5$

11. 12 ____ $3 = 15$

12. 9 ____ $2 = 7$

13. 9 ____ $4 = 36$

14. 14 ____ $2 = 16$

15. 19 ____ $1 = 18$

16. 30 ____ $5 = 6$

17. 4 ____ $3 = 12$

18. 18 ____ $6 = 24$

19. 60 ____ $10 = 6$

20. 9 ____ $0 = 9$

Name_____

Write the missing operation signs.

1. $12 \underline{\quad} 3 \underline{\quad} 2 = 17$

2. $45 \underline{\quad} 9 = 5$

3. $10 \underline{\quad} 3 = 3 \underline{\quad} 4$

4. $3 \underline{\quad} 5 = 10 \underline{\quad} 5$

5. $9 = 36 \underline{\quad} 4$

6. $24 \underline{\quad} 4 = 4 \underline{\quad} 5$

7. $50 \underline{\quad} 5 = 4 \underline{\quad} 6$

8. $32 = 4 \underline{\quad} 8$

9. $28 \underline{\quad} 4 = 24$

10. $6 \underline{\quad} 6 = 4 \underline{\quad} 9$

11. $45 \underline{\quad} 30 = 15$

12. $3 \underline{\quad} 6 \underline{\quad} 4 = 16 \underline{\quad} 3$

13. $60 = 6 \underline{\quad} 10$

14. $48 \underline{\quad} 6 = 8$

15. $15 \underline{\quad} 1 = 15$

16. $49 \underline{\quad} 8 = 41$

17. $16 \underline{\quad} 4 = 4$

18. $34 \underline{\quad} 7 = 41$

19. $34 = 41 \underline{\quad} 7$

20. $90 \underline{\quad} 13 = 103$

Name_____

Write the missing operation signs.

1. (3 ___ 2) ___ 4 = 10

2. 25 = 5 ___ (4 ___ 5)

3. 65 ___ 7 = 8 ___ 9

4. 46 ___ 6 = 8 ___ 5

5. 54 ___ 6 = 9 ___ 1

6. 9 ___ 5 = 50 ___ 5

7. 100 ___ 5 = 40 ___ 20

8. (42 ___ 2) ___ 5 = 9 ___ 5

9. (3 ___ 10) ___ 6 = 24

10. 9 = 81 ___ 9

11. (50 ___ 4) ___ 4 = 25 ___ 2

12. 6 = 72 ___ 12

13. (88 ___ 7) ___ 9 = 9

14. 60 ___ (12 ___ 3) = 8 ___ 8

15. 90 ___ 1 = (6 ___ 10) ___ 30

16. 1,000 ___ 4 = 4,000

17. 450 ___ 150 = (5 ___ 100) ___ 100

18. 345 ___ 455 = 400 ___ 2

19. (890 ___ 5) ___ 0 = 6,660 ___ 6,660

20. 6,900 ___ (50 ___ 50) = 3,400 ___ 3,400

Algebra

Objective
Solve word problems using equations.

Materials
- Copies of word problems for mini-lessons and group lessons
- Math notebooks
- Counters
- Activity sheets (pages 47–49)

Mini-Lesson

1. Give each student a copy of the following problem: "Ben was going to plant pumpkins. He bought 6 seed packets. Each packet contained 5 seeds. How many seeds did Ben have to plant?"
2. Ask students to solve the problem in their math notebooks. Before discussing the answer, write these equations on the board: $6 \times 5 = 30$, $6 + 5 = 11$, $6 - 5 = 1$, $30 \div 10 = 3$. Ask, "Which of these equations matches the word problem? How do you know?" Read the equation as, "Six packets times 5 seeds per packet equals 30 seeds."
3. Ask, "What operation is used for this problem? Why don't the other operations make sense?" Many students at this level pick the numbers from the story (5 and 6) and guess at what to do with them. Make a picture or highlight words in the problem to emphasize what it is asking. Then, show how to set up the equation to solve the problem.

Group 1 ○

Drawing Pictures to Solve Word Problems
1. Read the word problem: "Sally ran 6 laps at the track on Monday. On Tuesday, she ran 3 laps. How many laps did she run in all?"
2. Explain, "There is a girl at the track." Draw a stick figure and a running track on the board. "On Monday, she ran 6 laps." Circle the track 6 times with your hand. Have students place counters on their desks to mark each lap as you trace the track. "Then, she ran 3 laps on Tuesday." Demonstrate circling the track while students place counters in a different pile.
3. "The question asks how many laps she ran in all. What words tell which operation to use? Add $6 + 3$." Write the equation and read it as *6 laps plus 3 laps equals 9 laps in all*.
4. Continue with visual, concrete examples. Encourage students to draw or act out each problem.

Group 2 ▢

Clues for Solving Word Problems
1. Read the story problem with the group: "Markers come in packs of 10. If you bought 3 packs, how many markers would you have in total?" Have students solve the problem on their own in their math notebooks and list key words from the problem.
2. Explain to students that they should search for clues to help write an equation. Ask students to circle any important key words, such as *in total* and *packs of 10*, which signal multiplication. Demonstrate how to identify the numbers and key words in the problem. Work together to create a list of key words for each operation.
3. Use the key words to determine the number sentence needed to solve the problem. Ask, "Which operation did you use? What numbers did you combine? What was your final answer?"
4. Practice identifying key words in other word problems and writing the corresponding equations.

Group 3 △

Writing Word Problems
1. Write $(4 \times 12) + (3 \times 12) = 84$ on the board. Remind students that parentheses tell them what to do first in a problem.
2. Ask students to write a word problem to describe the equation. Say, "Multiplication deals with sets or groups of things. What things come in sets of 12? What word signals addition?" Write the example: "Kyle was baking cupcakes for the bake sale. He went to the store and bought 4 dozen eggs. When he got home, he realized he needed more. So, he went back and bought 3 more dozen. How many eggs did Kyle buy in all?" Ask students, "Which part of the story says to write 4×12? And 3×12? What words suggest using parentheses? Which part says to add the two amounts together?"
3. Direct students to write their own word problems for the same equation. Discuss students' stories. Have students find the clue words in their stories.
4. Continue writing word problems for other equations.

Name_____

Solve each problem. Show your work with pictures and equations.

1. Jayla and Trey picked some apples at the orchard. Jayla picked 12 apples. Trey picked 6. How many apples did they pick in all?

2. Six tricycles were lined up along the wall in the toy store. How many wheels were there in all?

3. In the pet store, there were 18 animals. There were 6 dogs and the rest were cats. How many cats were in the pet store?

4. Sam had 5 shoe boxes. In each box, there were 4 rocks. How many rocks did he have altogether?

5. Rosa wanted to share her snack between herself and her 2 friends. She had 21 grapes in her bag. How many grapes did each friend get?

Name_____

Solve each problem. Choose the number sentence that matches the story. Then, circle clue words to explain your answer.

1. Eight friends want to share 40 cookies evenly. How many cookies does each friend get?

   a. $40 \div 8 = 5$ b. $40 + 8 = 48$

   c. $40 - 8 = 32$ d. $40 \div 2 = 20$

2. The class was selling pizzas for a fund-raiser. Juan sold 15 pizzas. Mia sold 8 pizzas. Tony sold 22 pizzas. How many pizzas did Juan and Mia sell together?

   a. $22 \times 8 = 176$ b. $8 + 22 = 30$

   c. $15 + 8 = 23$ d. $15 + 8 + 22 = 45$

3. There were 9 pencils in each bag. The teacher had 9 bags. How many pencils did she have in all?

   a. $9 - 9 = 0$ b. $9 + 9 = 18$

   c. $1 \times 9 = 9$ d. $9 \times 9 = 81$

4. The bookstore had 16 copies of the new best seller. They sold 12 copies on the first day. How many copies of the book were left?

   a. $16 + 12 = 28$ b. $16 - 12 = 4$

   c. $16 \times 12 = 192$ d. $12 \div 6 = 2$

5. Lily bought new notebooks for the school year. The notebooks were sold in packs of 3. If she bought 3 packs of notebooks and 2 packs of pencils, how many notebooks did Lily buy in all?

   a. $3 + 3 = 6$ b. $3 \times 2 = 6$

   c. $3 \times 3 = 9$ d. $3 + 2 = 5$

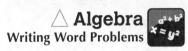

Name_____

Write a word problem to describe each equation.

1. 25 ÷ 5 = 5

_____

_____

_____

_____

2. (9 × 5) + 2 = 47

_____

_____

_____

_____

3. (10 × 4) + (2 × 5) = 50

_____

_____

_____

_____

4. 25 + (100 − 5) = 120

_____

_____

_____

_____

5. (580 − 30) + (25 × 3) = 625

_____

_____

_____

_____

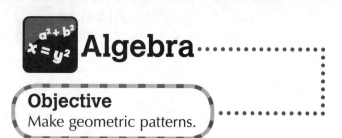

Algebra

Materials
- Pattern blocks
- Activity sheets (pages 51–53)

Objective
Make geometric patterns.

Mini-Lesson

1. Hand out pattern blocks. Draw the pattern *trapezoid, triangle, trapezoid, square, trapezoid, triangle, trapezoid, square* with shapes on the board. Ask students to replicate the pattern with their blocks.
2. What do students notice about these 8 shapes? Ask, "Do you see a pattern? What would the next 4 shapes be? If we gave each shape a letter, how could we show the pattern?" Write *ABAC* while pointing to each shape. "The *A* stands for the trapezoid. The triangle is the *B*," and so on.
3. Rearrange the blocks to follow the *ABCA* pattern. Ask, "What is the repeating section of the pattern? Which shape comes next in the pattern? Can you extend the pattern 2 times? How would you name the pattern using letters?"
4. Continue working with different patterns.

Group 1 ○

Extending Patterns with Blocks
1. Place the pattern blocks within students' reach. Draw shapes on the board to extend an *AB* pattern 3 times. Ask students to replicate this pattern with their blocks.
2. Instruct students to separate their patterns to show each repeated section, or pattern core. Ask, "What shapes are repeated? How many times are they repeated? Can you repeat the pattern 2 more times?" Then, extend the pattern with 4 more blocks.
3. Have students choose 3 shapes as the core of a new pattern. Have them repeat the core to extend the pattern 3 times.
4. Continue creating and extending different patterns. Encourage students to extend each other's patterns and work with increasingly more complex patterns.

Group 2 ▢

Translating and Extending Patterns
1. Write *ABCABC* on the board. Ask students to show the pattern with blocks. Ask, "How did you decide which shapes to put where? What are the rules of this pattern? Can you name the type of pattern using letters?" Discuss why letters are often used to represent patterns by naming the repeating section, or pattern core.
2. Ask, "What other things can we use to show this same pattern?" Have students draw the pattern with different graphic objects such as hearts, flowers, plus signs, arrows, etc.
3. Write *ABBCCA* on the board. Tell students, "Using just an arrow, draw this pattern so that it repeats 3 times. Will everyone have the same pictures? Will everyone have the same basic pattern?" Have students share their patterns and compare. Discuss using flips and turns of shapes to create the different items in a pattern.
4. Continue working with various patterns.

Group 3 △

Growing Patterns
1. On the board, draw 2 squares, then 4 squares (2 rows of 2), then 6 squares (3 rows of 2). Ask students to extend the pattern 3 more times.
2. Now, ask students to calculate how many squares would be in the 10th item. What about the 20th item? Ask, "How can this be solved without drawing the entire pattern?"
3. Show students how to make a table. One column should show the item number, and the second column should show how many squares are used. Figure out the rule. Explain, "The third item has 6 squares. The seventh item has 14 squares. Each item is multiplied by 2. How many squares does the 100th item have?"
4. Continue with other growing patterns.

Name_____

Circle the repeated section of each pattern. Extend the pattern 2 more times.

1. ◯△▢◯◯△▢◯ _____

2. ▢◯◇▢◯◇ _____

3. △▱▱△▱▱ _____

4. ◯◇◯◯◯◇◯◯ _____

5. ▢▢▢◯◯◯▢▢◯◯ _____

6. ▢△▢△ _____

7. ◇◯▢△◇◯▢△ _____

8. ◯▢▢◯◯▢▢◯ _____

9. ▱◯◯◇▱◯◯◇ _____

10. ◯◯▢◯◯◯▢ _____

Name_____

Draw a line to match each pattern to another with the same pattern type.

1. ⇧○◇⇧⇧○◇⇧   a. ☐☐◎☐☐◎

2. ◎☐◎◎◎☐☐◎◎   b. ✓•//✓•//

3. ∿∿••∿∿∿••   c. ☐○☐☐☐○☐☐

4. —○○——○○—   d. ◇▱○◇▱○

5. ⇩△☐⇩△☐   e. ☐◇◎☐☐◇◎☐

6. ◇◇◎◇◇◎   f. ⇩∿∿✗⇩∿∿✗

7. /☐☐•/☐☐•   g. ✓○✓☐✓○✓☐

8. △◇△⬡   h. ○⬡△△○⬡△△

9. ▱○//▱○//   i. •⋀⋀⋀•• ⋀⋀⋀•

10. ⋀⋀⋀○⋀⋀☐⋀⋀○⋀⋀☐   j. ◎✗◎✗

Name_____

Continue each pattern 2 times. Complete the chart to answer the questions.

1.

_____   _____

If the pattern was extended 10 times, how many squares would there be? _____

What is the rule? _____

How did you calculate your answer without drawing each item? _____

_____

item	number of squares

2.

_____   _____

If the pattern was extended 10 times, how many circles would there be? _____

What is the rule? _____

How did you calculate your answer without drawing each item? _____

_____

item	number of squares

3.

_____   _____

If the pattern was extended 10 times, how many sides would there be? _____

What is the rule? _____

How did you calculate your answer without drawing each item? _____

_____

item	number of squares

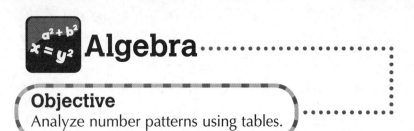 **Algebra**

Materials
• Activity sheets (pages 55–57)

Objective
Analyze number patterns using tables.

Mini-Lesson

1. Explain that the following chart is on the wall at a car repair shop. Draw a T-chart the with numbers *1, 2, 3,* and *4* in the left column and *$50, $100, $150,* and *$200* in the right column. Title the chart *Tires*. Ask students to explain what they think the chart means and how it is used.
2. Tell students that this chart is used for the price of tires. It is a handy reference for the owner to know how much to charge if someone orders more than 1 tire. "How much does each tire cost? That is the rule for this table. If someone orders 5 tires, how much does it cost? What about 10 tires? How can the cost be calculated?"
3. Ask students to demonstrate in numbers and pictures how they calculated the cost of 10 tires.
4. Continue working with other T-charts.

Group 1 ○
Introducing Charts

1. Draw a picture of 3 dogs. Ask, "If each dog has 4 legs, how many legs are in this picture?"
2. Ask, "What if 1 more dog arrives? How many legs would there be? What if there were 10 dogs?" Discuss strategies for calculating the answer. Students might draw pictures, continue counting, or add 4s.
3. Draw a T-chart that shows the number of dogs in the first column and the number of legs in the second column. Ask, "What operation is done to the number of dogs to find how many legs there are altogether? To solve for 5 dogs, I can multiply 5 times 4. Or, I can continue my pattern, counting by 4s (4, 8, 12, 16, 20). Do these strategies still work with 10 dogs? Twenty dogs?"
4. Continue with other examples. Encourage using concrete, visual strategies.

Group 2 ☐
Working with Number Patterns

1. Show students a T-chart with *1, 2, 3,* and *4* in the left column and *3, 6, 9,* and *12* in the right column. Ask what this chart could represent. Accept all reasonable answers. Suggest that these are wheels on a tricycle. "One tricycle has 3 wheels; 2 tricycles have 4 wheels; etc. Are the numbers on the right side greater or less than the numbers on the left side? What operations are used to make numbers larger? What is an addition rule for this chart? What is a multiplication rule for this chart?" (Each time, 3 is added to the number in the wheel column, or the number of tricycles is multiplied by 3.)
2. Ask students to continue this chart through 10 tricycles. Discuss how they found the answers.
3. Now, ask students to create charts of their own. Observe if students stay consistent with a rule and apply it to each number.
4. Have the group calculate the rules on each other's charts.

Group 3 △
Input/Output Charts

1. Draw an input/output chart on the board with inputs *20, 15, 10,* and *5* and outputs *4, 3, 2,* and *1*. Ask, "Are the numbers on the right greater or less than the numbers on the left? What operation can be applied to the numbers in the left column to get the numbers in the right column?"
2. Draw another input/output chart with four input numbers. Leave out two numbers on the input side, but provide the corresponding output numbers. Ask, "What is the rule for this input/output chart? How can you find the missing input numbers?"
3. Ask students to create their own input/output charts with at least five input numbers. Have them leave a few numbers off the chart to make it more difficult for the group to solve. Also, challenge students to write charts with two-step rules, such as *x 3 + 2*.
4. Have students share their charts and have other students calculate the rules.

CD-104563 © Carson-Dellosa

Name_____

Write the rule for each chart.

1. Rule: _____

Input	Output
4	14
8	18
10	20
55	65

2. Rule: _____

Input	Output
100	95
45	40
30	25
15	10

3. Rule: _____

Input	Output
3	12
8	17
11	20
20	29

4. Rule: _____

Input	Output
4	11
12	19
22	29
38	45

5. Rule: _____

Input	Output
15	12
24	21
32	29
54	51

6. Rule: _____

Input	Output
38	40
45	47
61	63
101	103

Name_____

Write the rule for each chart. Then, fill in the missing numbers. For numbers 7–8, create your own input/output charts.

1. Rule: _____

Input	Output
100	90
60	50
30	20
20	10

2. Rule: _____

Input	Output
125	140
170	___
305	320
380	___

3. Rule: _____

Input	Output
3	18
5	30
8	___
11	___

4. Rule: _____

Input	Output
245	___
550	575
810	835
925	___

5. Rule: _____

Input	Output
5	25
6	___
8	___
9	81

6. Rule: _____

Input	Output
45	195
150	300
240	___
300	___

7. Rule: _____

Input	Output

8. Rule: _____

Input	Output

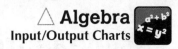
Name_____

Write the rule for each chart. Then, fill in the missing numbers. For numbers 7–8, create your own input/output charts.

1. Rule: _____

Input	Output
800	650
___	500
500	___
350	200

2. Rule: _____

Input	Output
34	68
42	84
68	___
___	162

3. Rule: _____

Input	Output
25	75
75	___
85	255
___	315

4. Rule: _____

Input	Output
40	402
50	502
60	602
70	___

5. Rule: _____

Input	Output
3	16
5	26
6	___
8	___

6. Rule: _____

Input	Output
700	350
___	250
300	150
___	50

7. Rule: _____

Input	Output

8. Rule: _____

Input	Output

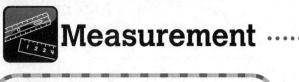

Measurement

Objective
Measure to the inch and the half inch.

Materials
- Rulers
- Buckets
- Various objects to measure
- Index cards
- Math notebooks
- Self-stick notes
- Construction paper
- Activity sheets (pages 59–61)

Mini-Lesson

1. Hand out rulers and buckets filled with objects to measure (paper clips, pencils, markers, staplers, index cards, business cards, etc.).
2. Teach students how to measure by lining an object up with the end of a ruler.
3. Ask students to measure the width of an index card (5 inches). Now, measure something that is *close* to an inch mark, such as a jumbo paper clip (about 2 inches). Explain that if an object measures close to one of the inches, students should round to the closest inch.
4. Measure something that ends near a half-inch mark, such as the width of a business card (3 1/2 inches). Explain that if an object falls halfway between two inch marks, we call it 1/2 inch.
5. Give students time to practice measuring objects.

Group 1 ◯

Observing while Measuring
1. Give students index cards to measure. Observe if they are lining up the rulers correctly and measuring accurately. Students tend to line up the ruler with the first inch, or they may not line it up exactly with the end of the ruler.
2. Demonstrate how to round to the nearest inch if an object does not line up exactly at an inch mark. Teach students how to find the half-inch mark.
3. Give students 5 objects to measure and record the lengths in their math notebooks. Then, compare the lengths and make sure they are measuring correctly. Observe where they are making mistakes and immediately correct their errors.

Group 2 ▢

Estimate, Then Measure
1. Give students time to practice measuring objects. Observe if they are lining up the end of the ruler correctly and measuring accurately.
2. Ask students to draw a line that is 1 inch long. Watch how they manipulate their rulers and make the lines. Check for accuracy.
3. Have students study their lines. Ask, "What is something that you have with you at all times or most of the time that is about 1 inch long?" Explain that a benchmark, such as the length of a finger or width of a thumb, can help when estimating lengths.
4. Give each student a self-stick note. First, have students estimate the length of one side of the note using their benchmarks. Then, have them record their estimates. Finally, ask them to measure.
5. Discuss, "How close was the estimate to the actual measurement? Why is estimating important? When can estimating measurements be useful?"

Group 3 △

Measuring for Accuracy
1. Give students time to practice measuring objects. Observe if they are lining up the end of the ruler correctly and measuring accurately.
2. Give students something longer than 12 inches to measure, such as a large sheet of construction paper. Ask, "What happens if the paper is longer than the ruler? How can we take an accurate measurement?"
3. Demonstrate how to line up the ruler and then move it to finish measuring. Give students a chance to practice with the construction paper.
4. Ask students to measure the desk, the tabletop, or the door width. Have them return to the group with their measurements. Then, compare and discuss the answers and the strategies that students used to measure.

Name_____

Measure the length of each object. Record the results.

1. _____ inches

2. _____ inches

3. _____ inches

4. _____ inches

5. _____ inches

6. _____ inches

7. _____ inches

8. _____ inches

9. _____ inches

10. _____ inches

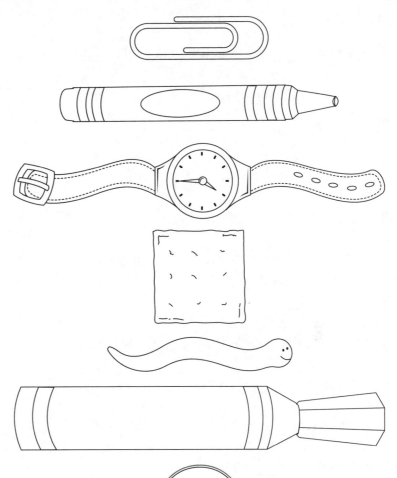

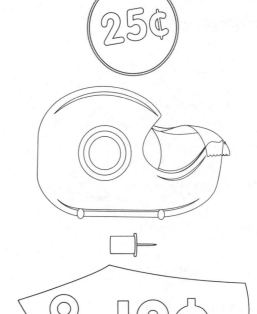

Name_____

Estimate the length of each object. Then, measure the object and record the results.

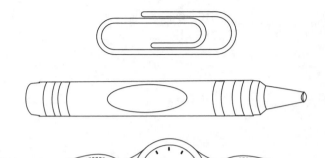

1. Estimate: _____ inches

   Actual measurement: _____ inches

2. Estimate: _____ inches

   Actual measurement: _____ inches

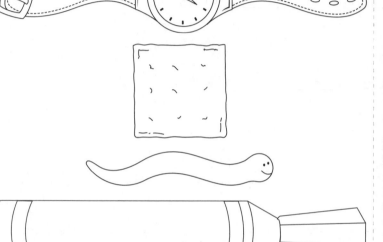

3. Estimate: _____ inches

   Actual measurement: _____ inches

4. Estimate: _____ inches

   Actual measurement: _____ inches

5. Estimate: _____ inches

   Actual measurement: _____ inches

6. Estimate: _____ inches

   Actual measurement: _____ inches

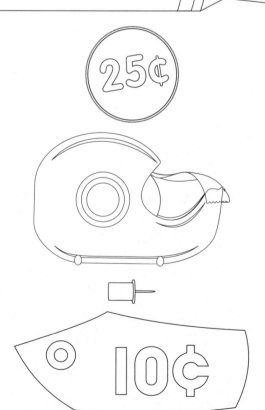

7. Estimate: _____ inches

   Actual measurement: _____ inches

8. Estimate: _____ inches

   Actual measurement: _____ inches

9. Estimate: _____ inches

   Actual measurement: _____ inches

10. Estimate: _____ inches

   Actual measurement: _____ inches

Name_____

Choose 10 classroom objects to measure. Estimate the measurement of each object. Measure. Record the measurement in the table below. Calculate the difference between the prediction and the actual measurement.

Object	Estimate	Measurement	Difference

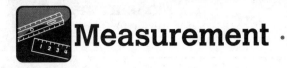

Measurement

Objective
Calculate perimeter and area.

Mini-Lesson

1. Give each student a sheet of graph paper. Explain that each square on the paper is 1 centimeter by 1 centimeter. Show students a drawing on graph paper of the rectangles with a perimeter of 12 centimeters (5 x 1, 4 x 2, 3 x 3).
2. Ask students to draw and label all of the rectangles by their arrays. Ask, "If you start at one corner of one of these rectangles and walk all the way around it along the border, how far would you walk?" Count the outside units of the rectangle and show how they add up to 12 centimeters. Explain that this is the *perimeter* of the rectangle, or the distance around. Write next to each array: *P (perimeter) = 12.*
3. Next, ask students to count the squares inside each rectangle. Explain that the area is the space inside the rectangle. It is written in square centimeters because you are counting the entire square as a unit. Write the area for each rectangle. For example, *A (area) = 5 square centimeters.*
4. Continue finding the area and perimeter of other rectangles.

Group 1 ○

Working with Blocks
1. Ask each student to use inch blocks to create a rectangle array that is 3 x 4. Ask, "How many blocks are in this rectangle? This space inside is the area. What is the area? Twelve square inches."
2. Now, ask students to count the outside sides of the blocks making up the rectangle (4 + 3 + 4 + 3). Say, "This distance around is the perimeter. This rectangle has a perimeter of 14 inches."
3. Draw a picture of the rectangle on the board. Show students how to add the outside lengths to find the perimeter and how to count the inside squares to find the area.
4. Continue working with the inch blocks. Ask students to find a perimeter: "Show me a rectangle with a perimeter of 18 inches." Then, ask them to find an area.

Group 2 ☐

Calculating Perimeter and Area
1. Give students graph paper. Ask them to draw all of the possible rectangles with a perimeter of 18 centimeters (1 x 8, 2 x 7, 3 x 6, 4 x 5).
2. Watch as students work to observe their strategies. Are they counting each line or writing number sentences? After drawing, ask students to explain their strategies and write equations to calculate the perimeter of *1 + 8 + 1 + 8.*
3. Ask students to calculate the areas of all of the rectangles. Once again, observe their processes. Are they counting each square unit, or are they multiplying the outside lengths? Teach students to multiply the length by the width to find the area. Draw some rectangles on plain paper and label them to find perimeter and area. Include rectangles labeled with only one width and one length and squares with only one side labeled.
4. Continue finding areas and perimeters of various rectangles.

Group 3 △

Perimeter and Area of Irregular Figures
1. Draw an irregular figure with multiple sides and angles on graph paper. A good example is a block letter *E*. Ask students to determine the area and perimeter of the shape.
2. Draw a similar irregular figure on plain paper. Label a few of the sides but not all of them. Ask, "What do you need to know to find the perimeter of this shape? How can the given measurements help you determine the missing ones?" Help students add, subtract, and compare the known measurements to calculate all of the side lengths and determine the perimeter of the shape.
3. Now, ask, "How can we find the area?" Show students how to divide irregular figures into rectangular sections. Find the areas of the smaller sections and add them together to find the total area of the irregular figure.
4. Challenge students to draw their own irregular figures, label only a few sides, and trade with partners to solve for perimeter and area.

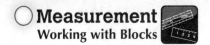
Name_____

Find the area and the perimeter of each rectangle.

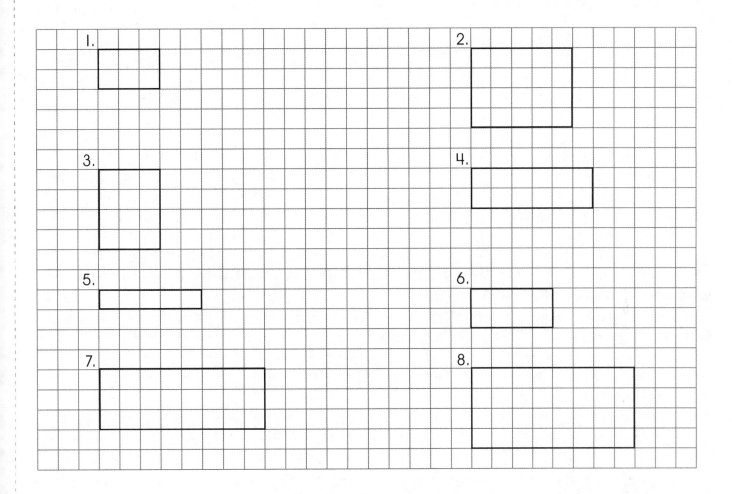

1. Area = _____ square units

   Perimeter = _____ units

2. Area = _____ square units

   Perimeter = _____ units

3. Area = _____ square units

   Perimeter = _____ units

4. Area = _____ square units

   Perimeter = _____ units

5. Area = _____ square units

   Perimeter = _____ units

6. Area = _____ square units

   Perimeter = _____ units

7. Area = _____ square units

   Perimeter = _____ units

8. Area = _____ square units

   Perimeter = _____ units

Name_____

Draw all of the possible rectangles that have a perimeter of 24. Inside each rectangle, write the area.

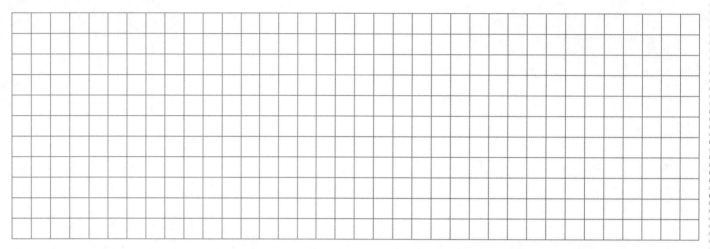

Draw all of the possible rectangles that have a perimeter of 30. Inside each rectangle, write the area.

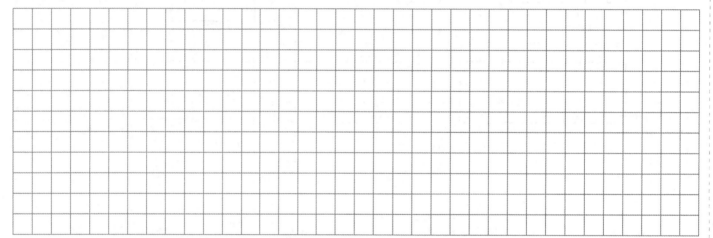

Calculate the area and the perimeter of each rectangle.

1. Area = _____

   Perimeter = _____

3 cm
5 cm | 5 cm
3 cm

3. Area = _____

   Perimeter = _____

9 mm
4 mm

2. Area = _____

   Perimeter = _____

4 in.
2 in. | 2 in.
4 in.

4. Area = _____

   Perimeter = _____

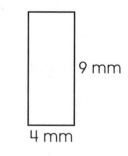

7 ft.
7 ft.

64

Name_____

Find the area and the perimeter of each figure.

1.
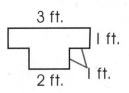

2.
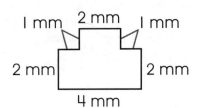
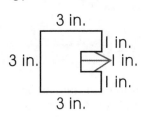

3.

4.
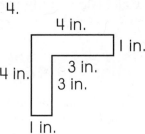

5.
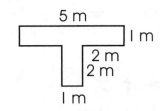

6.
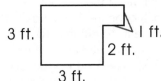
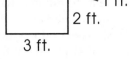

7.
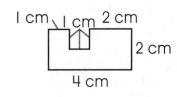

8.
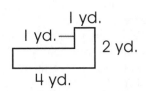

9.

10.
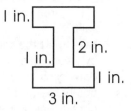

1. Area = _____

   Perimeter = _____

2. Area = _____

   Perimeter = _____

3. Area = _____

   Perimeter = _____

4. Area = _____

   Perimeter = _____

5. Area = _____

   Perimeter = _____

6. Area = _____

   Perimeter = _____

7. Area = _____

   Perimeter = _____

8. Area = _____

   Perimeter = _____

9. Area = _____

   Perimeter = _____

10. Area = _____

   Perimeter = _____

Measurement

Objective
Calculate volume of solid figures.

Materials
- Centimeter and inch cubes
- Math notebooks
- Small empty boxes, such as checkbook boxes
- Paper
- Pencils
- Activity sheets (pages 67–69)

Mini-Lesson

1. Distribute centimeter cubes to each student. Say, "Create a three-dimensional solid cube using your centimeter cubes. Make the dimensions 3 x 3 x 3. Calculate how many centimeter cubes are used to create this solid without taking the solid apart and counting each cube."
2. Discuss strategies for their calculations. Students might count all of the outside cubes and guess what is on the inside. They might say that there are 9 cubes on each layer and that there are 3 layers of cubes. Write down all of their strategies.
3. Have them take apart their solids and count each cube to confirm an answer.
4. Explain that they are finding *volume* (V), the area inside a solid object. Demonstrate the formula for volume (length x width x height) and how it works with the solid they just made.

Group 1
Using Cubes to Calculate Volume
1. Have each student create a three-dimensional solid with sides 4 x 2 and 3 units tall. Ask students to estimate how many cubes are used to create this solid.
2. Take apart the solids layer by layer. First, have students draw each layer in their math notebooks and label the dimensions. For example, the top layer is a rectangle that is 4 x 2. Then, have students remove the first layer to reveal the second layer, also 4 x 2, then the third layer, 4 x 2.
3. Write the equation of how many cubes make up the solid: *8 + 8 + 8 = 24*.
4. Show students the formula *length x width x height*. Ask, "How did we discover this without the formula? Each layer was 4 x 2, and we added the layers 3 times."

Group 2
Calculating Volume
1. Show students a small, empty box. Explain that you want to find how many cubes will fit inside the box, which is the volume of the box. Place an inch cube inside the box and ask students to estimate the volume, using the cube as a reference.
2. Next, have students calculate the actual volume of the box. Show how to measure the length and the width of the box. Trace the bottom of the box on paper. Then, measure and label the sides. Explain that this measurement is the area of one layer of the box. Ask, "What part of the box do we need to measure to determine the number of layers in the box?" Point out that the box has a height. Measure the height.
3. Ask, "Now that we have the number of layers in the box and the area of one layer, how do we determine the total area of the box?" Show the formula for volume: length x width x height.
4. Allow students to continue measuring different boxes and calculating their volumes.

Group 3
Calculating Volume from Sketches
1. Show a drawing of a rectangular prism that is 5 x 4 x 3. Ask students to calculate its volume.
2. Observe as they work. Which students are drawing sketches? Which are using repeated addition? Which are using multiplication? Discuss their strategies and calculate the final answer. Ask, "What kinds of measurements are needed to calculate volume? How are area and volume different? How are they alike?"
3. Help students draw sketches of cubes and rectangular prisms in their notebooks. Ask, "How are we able to show all of the sides?"
4. Divide students into pairs and give each pair a box. Have the pairs draw sketches of the boxes, measure and record the dimensions, and calculate the volumes. (Direct students to round measurements to the nearest whole numbers.) Discuss their processes and results.
5. Let students share their boxes with the group and tell their volumes. Challenge students to guess the dimensions of the boxes based on the given volumes.

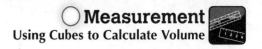
Name_____

Calculate the volume for each solid. Show your work.

1.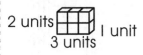
2 units 3 units 1 unit

2.
3 units 4 units 2 units

3.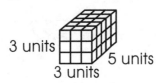
3 units 3 units 5 units

4.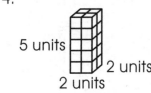
5 units 2 units 2 units

5.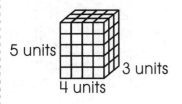
5 units 4 units 3 units

6.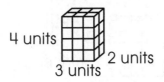
4 units 3 units 2 units

7.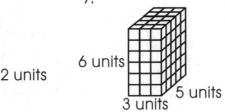
6 units 3 units 5 units

8.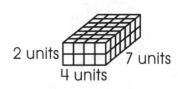
2 units 4 units 7 units

9.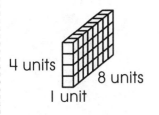
4 units 1 unit 8 units

10.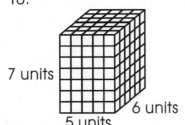
7 units 5 units 6 units

1. Volume = _____ cubic units   2. Volume = _____ cubic units

3. Volume = _____ cubic units   4. Volume = _____ cubic units

5. Volume = _____ cubic units   6. Volume = _____ cubic units

7. Volume = _____ cubic units   8. Volume = _____ cubic units

9. Volume = _____ cubic units   10. Volume = _____ cubic units

Name_____

Calculate the volume for each solid. Show your work.

1.
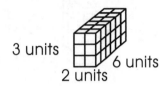
3 units
2 units
6 units

2.
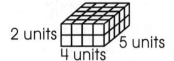
2 units
4 units
5 units

3.
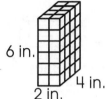
6 in.
2 in.
4 in.

4.
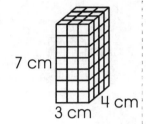
7 cm
3 cm
4 cm

5.
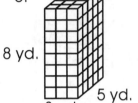
8 yd.
3 yd.
5 yd.

6.
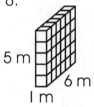
5 m
1 m
6 m

7.
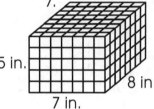
5 in.
7 in.
8 in.

8.
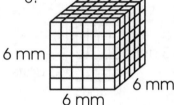
6 mm
6 mm
6 mm

9.
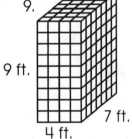
9 ft.
4 ft.
7 ft.

10.
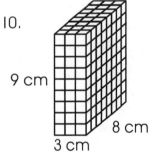
9 cm
3 cm
8 cm

1. Volume = _____

2. Volume = _____

3. Volume = _____

4. Volume = _____

5. Volume = _____

6. Volume = _____

7. Volume = _____

8. Volume = _____

9. Volume = _____

10. Volume = _____

Name_____

Sketch and label a box with each set of given dimensions. Calculate the volume of the box. Write the equation you used. Show your work.

1. 2 × 6 × 3	2. 4 × 5 × 5
Volume: _____	Volume: _____
3. 6 × 1 × 4	4. 8 × 3 × 3
Volume: _____	Volume: _____

Label the rectangular prisms with their dimensions.

5. Volume = 60

Length: _____

Width: _____

Height: _____

6. Volume = 45

Length: _____

Width: _____

Height: _____

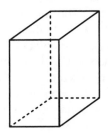

7. Volume = 24

Length: _____

Width: _____

Height: _____

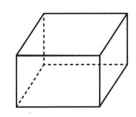

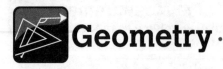

Geometry

Objective
Identify and describe polygons.

Materials
- Chart paper
- Math notebooks
- Pattern blocks
- Index cards
- Paper bag
- Activity sheets (pages 71–73)

Mini-Lesson

1. On chart paper, create a poster with the new vocabulary words for this lesson: *sides, vertex (vertices), polygon, trapezoid, triangle, rhombus, square, parallelogram, rectangle, pentagon, hexagon, octagon,* and *parallel*. Use the vocabulary words throughout the lesson and encourage students to use the correct terminology.
2. Ask each student to choose a pattern block of one of the shapes above. Discuss each shape's attributes.
3. Create a poster with students. Draw a sketch of each polygon on the poster. Label the sides and vertices. Write words to describe them, such as *parallel sides, equal length,* and *right angles*. Reference places that these shapes are seen in everyday life. Have students draw sketches and take notes in their math notebooks.

Group 1

Noticing Details

1. Give each student a trapezoid pattern block. Ask students to spend 3 minutes writing about their blocks. Ask, "What do you notice about the trapezoid? What makes it unique from other shapes? How many sides and vertices does it have?"
2. As students write, observe the vocabulary they use and their levels of detail. Use words such as *parallel, sides, vertices,* and *congruent* during a discussion. After the discussion, ask students to write for 3 more minutes using correct terminology. Continue the same activity with other blocks.
3. Now, put all of the blocks in a paper bag. Pull out 1 shape without letting the group see. Use geometric vocabulary to describe it and have students guess the shape.

Group 2

Geometric Vocabulary

1. For many students, the most difficult part of the geometry strand is learning vocabulary. Many of these words are not used in everyday conversation (*parallel, polygon, vertex,* etc.). So, it is important to reinforce the vocabulary by saying it, hearing it, and seeing it.
2. Have students create a set of vocabulary flash cards. Write each vocabulary word on one side of an index card and draw a sketch and write a short description of the word on the other side. For example, *four equal sides, no right angles* for a rhombus.
3. Have students study their cards and quiz each other. Then, use vocabulary words to give them step-by-step directions to draw shapes. For example, say, "Draw a shape that has 4 sides." Students may not all draw the same shape. Then, give another direction: "This shape has 4 right angles." Students should change their shapes to reflect the new information. Continue until all of the details are given. Check students' drawings to see if they drew the correct shape.

Group 3

Diagramming Attributes

1. Ask students to draw 3 large overlapping circles to form a Venn diagram. Have them refer to the vocabulary words used during the mini-lesson and on the poster. Have students choose 3 attributes (such as parallel lines, congruent sides, and right angles) and label each circle with one of the attributes.
2. Have students write the names of the polygons that fit into each category inside the circles. Polygons that fit into more than one category should be written inside overlapping sections.
3. Have students continue making diagrams with other attributes or try including more circles in the diagrams.
4. Let students share their diagrams when they are complete.

Name_____

Draw a line to match each polygon to its name.

1.   a. trapezoid

2.   b. triangle

3. 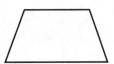   c. rhombus

4.    d. square

5.   e. parallelogram

6. 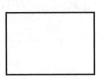   f. rectangle

7.   g. pentagon

8.   h. hexagon

9. 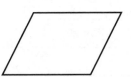   i. octagon

Name _____

Solve each riddle by matching the polygon description with its name.

Word Bank		
octagon	pentagon	trapezoid
parallelogram	rhombus	triangle

1. I am a polygon with 4 sides. I have 2 pairs of parallel sides. My sides all have equal lengths. I have no right angles. What am I? _____

2. I have an odd number of sides. I have more than 3 sides, but less than half a dozen. What am I? _____

3. I am a polygon with 4 vertices. None of my sides form a right angle. I have one pair of parallel lines. What am I? _____

4. I am a polygon. Sometimes, I am called by a more specific name such as *rhombus* or *rectangle*. I have 2 pairs of parallel sides. What am I? _____

5. The number of my sides is a multiple of 4. Forty divided by 5 equals how many sides I have. What am I? _____

6. I have an odd number of vertices. I am one of the shapes that makes up a square pyramid. What am I? _____

Write your own polygon riddles.

7. _____

_____

8. _____

_____

9. _____

_____

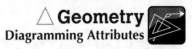

Name_____

List correct polygon names under each category in the chart.

Parallel Lines	Right Angles	Congruent Sides	Odd Number of Vertices	Even Number of Sides

 # Geometry

Objective
Identify and describe geometric solids.

Materials
- Wooden solids
- Everyday objects
- Old magazines
- Scissors
- Glue
- Construction paper
- Math notebooks
- Toilet paper rolls
- Tape
- Activity sheets (pages 75–77)

Mini-Lesson

1. Provide sets of wooden solids as well as various everyday objects in the shapes of the geometric solids: cones (ice-cream cones and funnels), cylinders (soup cans and toilet paper rolls), rectangular prisms (cereal boxes and shoe boxes), spheres (basketballs and globes), and cubes (dice).
2. Give students time to explore the objects. Ask students to match the wooden solids with everyday objects. Encourage using vocabulary such as *parallel, perpendicular, edges, vertices, and face.*
3. Distribute magazines and have students cut out photographs in the shapes of solids. For example, cut out an ottoman in the shape of a cube. Have students glue the pictures on construction paper and label the various solids.

Group 1 ◯

Exploring Faces
1. Provide wooden sets of solids. Ask students to identify the name of each solid.
2. Allow time for students to explore the solids. Encourage them to look at all of the sides and talk about what they notice. Encourage using vocabulary such as *faces, edges, vertices, parallel, and perpendicular.*
3. Ask each student to take a square pyramid and trace all of the faces of the solid. Discuss how many faces it has and the name of each face.
4. Continue with other solids. If students are confused by the surfaces of a cone, cylinder, or sphere, emphasize that faces are flat surfaces that can be traced as two-dimensional shapes.

Group 2 ▢

Studying Solids
1. Give each student a rectangular prism. Choose a wooden solid, a cereal box, or a shoe box. Allow time for students to study and casually discuss the prisms as a group.
2. Ask students to draw sketches of their prisms. Show the group how to draw a three-dimensional figure. Then, have them count the faces of the solid. Encourage them to turn it to see many different angles.
3. Have students write the number of faces on the prism in their math notebooks. Next, have them draw and label all of the different faces that make up the solid. Then, have them count and record the vertices and the edges. Ask students to write 3 sentences about the solid. Encourage them to use the vocabulary words.
4. Continue with other solids.

Group 3 △

Creating Nets
1. Give each student a wooden cylinder. Have students study the solid from all angles. Encourage the use of appropriate mathematical vocabulary.
2. Discuss how to represent this three-dimensional figure as a two-dimensional pattern. Have students trace either end of a toilet paper roll on paper separated by the length of the tube.
3. Ask, "How can we show the rest of this solid on the paper?" Use a toilet paper roll as a real-life example of a cylinder. Cut the roll lengthwise. Flatten it to show it is a rectangle. Trace it on the paper between the 2 circles. Explain to students that they just made a "net" of a cylinder.
4. Ask, "How can we turn this pattern back into a cylinder?" Cut out the shapes, keeping them connected at a small point. Tape the rectangle into a tube. Fold the circles over the ends and tape them down.
5. Create other solids with nets.

Name_____

Draw a line from each solid to every two-dimensional shape that is a face on the solid.

1.
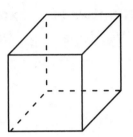

a.
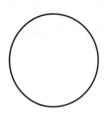

2.
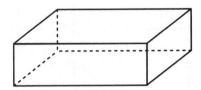

b.

3.
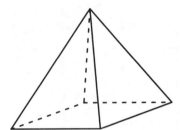

c.

4.
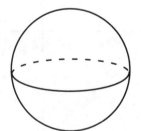

d.
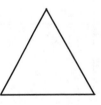

5.
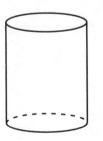

e.   no faces

6.
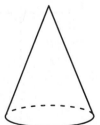

Name_____

Complete the chart.

Picture of Solid	Name of Solid	Number of Faces	Number of Edges	Number of Vertices	Examples in Real Life

Name_____

Draw a line to match each net to the correct solid.

1.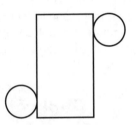

a.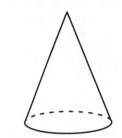

2.

b.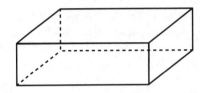

3.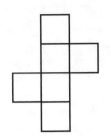

c.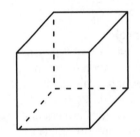

4.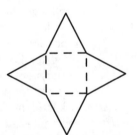

d.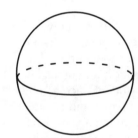

5.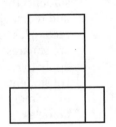

e.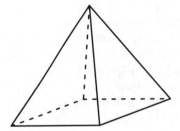

6.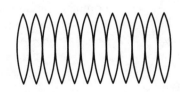

f.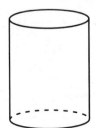

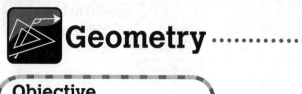

Geometry

Materials
- Construction paper
- Graph paper
- Rulers
- Index cards
- Activity sheets (pages 79–81)

Objective
Identify attributes of triangles.

Mini-Lesson

1. Distribute construction paper and ask each student to cut out a triangle. Tape the triangles on the chart paper.
2. Study the triangles with students. Ask, "What is the same about all of these shapes? How are they different?" Then, develop a definition of a triangle. For example, a triangle has 3 sides, 3 angles, and 3 vertices.
3. Measure and record the lengths of the sides of a few triangles. Introduce the terms *isosceles, scalene,* and *equilateral.* Label the triangles. (If there are no examples of one of the types, make one to include.)
4. Next, discuss angles. Show students an example of a right angle. Then, compare it to obtuse and acute angles. Explain that triangles can also be named by their angles. Label the triangles with the correct angle names.

Group 1 ○

Drawing Triangles
1. Describe the different types of triangles: equilateral (all of the sides are equal), scalene (all of the sides are different), and isosceles (two sides are equal). Give students time to practice identifying different types of triangles.
2. Next, discuss angles. Show students the corner of a sheet of construction paper and explain that the corner is a right angle. Have each student trace a corner of a sheet of paper and create a triangle from the angle. Teach obtuse (greater than 90°) and acute (less than 90°) angles.
3. Have students draw the different types of triangles using graph paper and rulers. Have students use the graph paper units as a guide for measuring side lengths and creating different angles. After drawing, have students label their triangles with the vocabulary words.

Group 2 □

Naming Triangles
1. Review the definitions of the different types of triangles and angles: scalene, equilateral, isosceles, right, obtuse, and acute.
2. Draw a triangle on the board and ask students to describe it. "How would we label this triangle if we only looked at the lengths of the sides? How would we label it when looking at just the angles?" Explain that some people have many names (daughter, sister, niece), depending on the relationship we look at. It is the same with triangles.
3. Play a game with students. Write the words *scalene, equilateral, isosceles, right, obtuse,* and *acute* on index cards and place them on a table. Divide the group into two teams. Have one student from each team stand in front of the table. Hold up a picture of a triangle. As quickly as possible, each standing student should grab a card that describes the triangle. Because triangles can be described in more than one way, it is possible for both teams to win a point.
4. Continue playing until all types of triangles are identified and all students take a turn.

Group 3 △

Rules for Triangles
1. Review the definitions of the different types of triangles and angles: scalene, equilateral, isosceles, right, obtuse, and acute.
2. Let students experiment with drawing two types of triangles in one shape. For example, challenge students to draw a scalene right triangle; is it possible? How about an equilateral obtuse triangle? Discuss which combinations are and are not possible.
3. Ask students how squares and rectangles are related. Tell students the rule about squares and rectangles: "All squares are rectangles, but not all rectangles are squares." Ask, "What rules apply to types of triangles?" Let students use their drawing experiment to make up rules for triangles.
4. Let students share their rules. Discuss why certain combinations are necessary and why some are impossible.

Name_____

Draw a line to match each triangle to its name.

1. 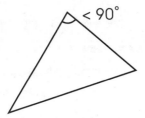   a. right triangle

2. 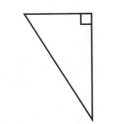   b. acute triangle

3. 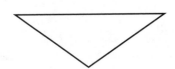   c. obtuse triangle

_____

4.    a. equilateral triangle

5.    b. isosceles triangle

6. 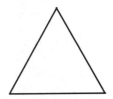   c. scalene triangle

Name_____

Label each triangle with two different names that can be used to describe it.

Word Bank		
right triangle acute triangle	obtuse triangle equilateral triangle	isosceles triangle scalene triangle

1. _____ _____

2. _____ _____

3. _____ _____

4. _____ _____

5. _____ _____

6. _____ _____

7. _____ _____

8. _____ _____

80

Name_____

Follow the directions.

1. Triangles can be described by the lengths of their sides: equilateral, scalene, or isosceles. Triangles can be described by their angles: acute, obtuse, or right. Choose a length descriptor and an angle descriptor.

_____   _____

2. Draw a triangle that fits **both** descriptions.

3. Explain why your triangle is both types. _____

_____

_____

_____

_____

_____

_____

Data Analysis & Probability

Materials
- Self-stick notes
- Math notebooks
- Index cards
- Dice
- Activity sheets (pages 83–85)

Objective
Collect and represent data in a line plot graph.

Mini-Lesson

1. Give each student a self-stick note with a large *X* drawn on it. Draw a horizontal line on the board labeled with the numbers 0 to 10 underneath.
2. Explain that you are doing a survey to find how many pets students have at home. You are going to collect the data and organize it on a line plot graph.
3. Have students place their notes along the line above the numbers representing how many pets they have at home. Make sure students carefully place their notes above each other.
4. Discuss the graph. Ask, "What kind of information is represented on this graph? Does it tell us what types of pets people have? How many pets do most people have? What is the fewest number of pets people have?"
5. Have students draw the graph in their math notebooks and write several statements about the data. Let students share their statements.

Group 1 ○

Representing Data in a Line Plot

1. Draw a tally chart on the board labeled *Favorite Number* (0, 1, 2, 3, 4, 5, 6, 7, 8, 9) and *Number of Teachers* (in tallies: 4, 3, 1, 6, 3, 2, 0, 6, 3, 2). Explain that you surveyed the teachers, and these are their favorite numbers.
2. Draw a number line labeled with numbers 0 to 9 on the board. Title it *Teachers' Favorite Numbers*. Assign each student a number along the number line and have him draw the correct number of X's above his number based on the information in the tally chart.
3. Discuss the completed line plot. Ask questions such as, "Which number or numbers did most teachers like best? Did more teachers like 2 or 9? Were there any numbers that no teachers chose?"
4. Ask students to draw the line plot in their math notebooks. Emphasize having a title, evenly spacing the numbers on a horizontal line, and drawing the X's directly above one another and aligning them horizontally.

Group 2 □

Collecting Data in a Line Plot

1. Draw a number line labeled with numbers 1 to 6 on the board. Let students take turns rolling a die and drawing an X along the number line to record the results of their rolls. Roll the die at least 10 times.
2. Teach these vocabulary words: *range* (difference between the greatest number and the least number), *mode* (the number that occurs most often), and *median* (the middle number when data is arranged from least to greatest).
3. Ask students to find the range, mode, and median of the data. Ask, "How can the line plot be used to determine the range? How can the mode of the data quickly be determined using a line plot? How does a line plot help to easily see the median? Is the median necessarily the same as the middle number along the number line of the line plot?"
4. Have students repeat the experiment on their own and record 10 trials on a line plot in their math notebooks. Have them analyze the data using the statistics of range, mode, and median.

Group 3 △

Analyzing Line Plot Data

1. Use the graph from the mini-lesson to gather and analyze data. First, have the group draw the line plot in their math notebooks.
2. Introduce *range* (difference between the greatest number and the least number), *mode* (the number that occurs most often), *median* (the middle number when the data is arranged from least to greatest), *mean* (the average), *gap* (spaces or blanks in the data), and *outlier* (any data that is outside the range of most of the data).
3. Use the data from the graph to find each of these statistics. Then, have students use the information to analyze the data. Ask, "What is an outlier? How does it affect the mean? How does the mode compare to the mean and the average? What can a gap tell us about the data?"
4. Discuss, "What is the importance of understanding *mean* or *range* when studying data? How can representing data in a line plot make analyzing statistics easier?"

Name_____

Show the data on each line plot. Then, answer the questions using the line plots.

GRAPH 1:
Ages of Kids in Class

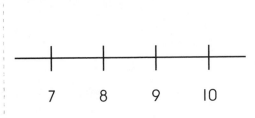

Age	Kids
7	I
8	TH II
9	TH I
10	II

1. How many students are 8 years old? _____

2. What age are the least number of students? _____

3. What age are the greatest number of students? _____

4. How many 8- and 9-year-olds are there in this class? _____

GRAPH 2:
Class Quiz Scores

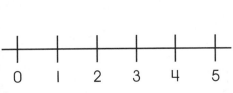

Age	Kids
0	
1	I
2	I
3	IIII
4	TH I
5	TH III

5. What number of points was scored by no students? _____

6. How many students scored 3 or fewer points? _____

7. How many more students scored 4 points than 1 point? _____

8. How many students are in this class altogether? _____

GRAPH 3:
Books Read Last Month

Age	Kids
0	III
1	IIII
2	TH
3	IIII
4	III
5	II

9. How many kids read 5 books? _____

10. How many kids read at least 2 books?

_____

11. How many more kids read 1 book than read 5 books? _____

12. What number of books did most kids read? _____

GRAPH 4:
Times Visited the Zoo

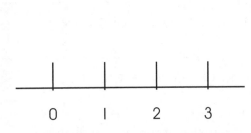

Age	Kids
0	IIII
1	TH I
2	III
3	II

13. How many students visited the zoo 3 times? _____

14. How many students have never been to the zoo? _____

15. How many students have visited the zoo 2 or more times? _____

16. How many students were surveyed for this line plot graph? _____

Write the numbers 0 to 9 on index cards. Place them facedown and draw a card at random. Record your result on the line plot. Replace the card and repeat 20 times. Answer the questions about your line plot.

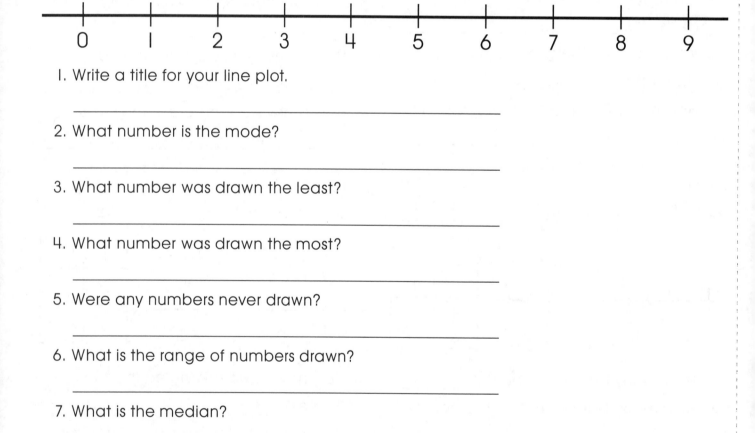

1. Write a title for your line plot.

   _____

2. What number is the mode?

   _____

3. What number was drawn the least?

   _____

4. What number was drawn the most?

   _____

5. Were any numbers never drawn?

   _____

6. What is the range of numbers drawn?

   _____

7. What is the median?

   _____

8. How can showing data in a line plot make answering these questions easier?

   _____

   _____

   _____

Name_____

Think of a survey question to ask the class, such as, "How many people live in your house?" If a survey is not possible, research a question such as, "How many pages do the fiction books in the classroom contain?" Collect data in a tally chart. Organize the data on a line plot graph. Answer the questions about the data. Write 3 observations about the data.

Survey question: _____

_____

What is the range? _____   What is the mean? _____

What is the mode? _____   Are there any outliers? _____

What is the median? _____   Are there any gaps? _____

Observations about data:

1. _____

2. _____

3. _____

Data Analysis & Probability

Materials
- Self-stick notes
- Math notebooks
- Chart paper
- Activity sheets (pages 87–89)

Objective
Collect and represent data in a bar graph.

Mini-Lesson

1. Give each student a self-stick note. Ask each student to draw a picture of how she got to school this morning (bus, walk, car ride) on the note. Have students randomly place the notes on the board.
2. Explain that the notes are the collected data for a graph. Now, the data needs to be organized.
3. Demonstrate how to include a title, labels for the vertical and horizontal axis lines, and labels for the columns. Show how to organize the data by putting the notes in categories and then placing them neatly on the graph, forming columns.
4. Discuss, "How did the majority of students get to school? How many students rode the bus? What was the way the least amount of kids came to school? If we lived in another part of the country, would our data change?"

Group 1 ○

Creating a Graph Together
1. Use self-stick notes with the group. Have students label each note with a student's name from the class. Then, have them color the notes red (boy) or blue (girl).
2. Ask students to organize the data into categories.
3. Model how to draw a graph. Have students draw their own graphs in their math notebooks. Label the graph with a title, label the axes, and write labels for columns. Show how to make columns to represent the data.
4. Ask students to make observations about the data on the graph. Say, "According to this graph, most of the kids in our class are boys. There are 4 more boys than girls. I wonder if other classes have more boys than girls."

Group 2 □

Working with Data
1. Bring in a book of world records or an almanac. Find an interesting topic to graph, such as fastest animals. Before they read further, ask students to predict which animal is the fastest and how fast it can move.
2. Have students record and organize the information in their math notebooks. Create a bar graph as a group. Study the data and decide how to best represent it. Ask, "What will the scale of the graph be? What intervals will the numbers be on the vertical axis?" Label the axes.
3. Find the range, mode, and median of the data together.
4. Discuss, "Were our predictions close to the actual data? What did we learn about animals? Was there anything that surprised us about the results?"

Group 3 △

Representing Data in Multiple Ways
1. Use the data from the mini-lesson. During the mini-lesson, students made a vertical bar graph. Explain that there are many ways to represent data.
2. Ask, "What other ways are there to illustrate the findings?" Discuss horizontal and vertical bar graphs, line plots, line graphs, pictographs, tally charts, and tables.
2. Create each type of graph together. Ask, "Are there some that are better than others? Can we display all of the information on every kind of graph? Which graphs are easier to understand? What are the pros and cons of each one? Why would someone choose one graph over another?"
4. On chart paper, create a poster of the various ways to represent the same data.

Name_____

Use the information in each T-chart to complete the bar graph. Then, answer questions about the graph.

Favorite School Lunch

Lunches	Number of Kids
lasagna	卌
sub sandwich	卌 ||
grilled cheese	|||
pizza	卌 卌

1. How many students like sub sandwiches best? _____

2. What lunch choice is the overall favorite? _____

3. What lunch choice do the fewest number of students like?_____

_____

4. How many students were asked about their favorite school lunch? _____

Favorite Summer Activity

Activity	Number of Kids
swimming	卌 ||
baseball	||||
soccer	卌
tennis	||

5. How many students like baseball? _____

6. What activity do most students like the best? _____

7. How many students like soccer or baseball? _____

8. What activity had the fewest number of kids who liked it?_____

Name_____

Use the information in each T-chart to complete the bar graph. Then, answer questions about the graph.

Number of Kids in Each Grade	
Grade Level	Number of Kids
1st grade	55
2nd grade	85
3rd grade	70
4th grade	55
5th grade	90

1. What is the median? _____

2. What is the mode? _____

3. What is the range? _____

4. Write 3 observations about the data represented in the graph.

_____

_____

Tickets Sold to Baseball Game	
Month	Tickets Sold
May	400
June	400
July	700
August	600
September	250

5. What is the median? _____

6. What is the mode? _____

7. What is the range? _____

8. Write 3 observations about the data represented in the graph.

_____

_____

_____

Name_____

Answer the questions. Using the data provided and your answers to the questions, draw the best type of graph to display each set of data.

Reading Choices
in Library

Choices	Number of Kids
Picture Books	400
Chapter Books	750
Nonfiction	800
Magazines	150

1. What intervals would be best in order to show this data? _____

_____

2. Is a tally chart a good choice to display this data? Explain. _____

_____

3. Can this data be shown with a line plot? Why or why not? _____

_____

4. Would a vertical or horizontal bar graph be better? Explain. _____

_____

Eye Color

Color	Number of Kids
brown	‖‖‖ ‖‖
blue	‖‖‖
green	‖
hazel	‖‖‖

5. What is the greatest number of data in a category? _____

_____

6. Would a table or a bar graph be more helpful to compare results? Explain._____

_____

7. Could this information be plotted in a line graph? Why or why not?_____

_____

8. If this data were represented in a pictograph, what would be a good symbol to use?

_____

Data Analysis & Probability

Objective
Conduct probability experiments and represent data.

Materials
- Paper bag
- Colored counters
- Spinners from board games
- Paper clips
- Crayons
- Activity sheets (pages 91–93)
- Math notebooks
- Pencils

Mini-Lesson

1. Show students an empty paper bag. Place 10 counters (9 red and 1 blue) inside the bag.
2. Ask, "What are the chances that the first counter picked will be red? Is it certain (for sure)? Likely (probably will happen)? Unlikely (probably will not happen)? Or impossible (no chance)? Have students record their predictions in their math notebooks.
3. Pull out one counter. Record the color on a tally chart. Return the counter to the bag and repeat 10 times.
4. Discuss the results and compare them to students' predictions. Ask, "What would happen if the experiment was repeated 100 times? Would the data remain the same or change dramatically? What is the likelihood of pulling a yellow counter from the bag? How could the chance of pulling a yellow counter be changed?"

Group 1 ○

Testing Spinners
1. Draw a circle and divide it into 4 equal sections. Color each section a different color. Demonstrate how to make a spinner. Hold a pencil at the center of the circle, holding a paper clip in place. Flick the paper clip so that it spins around the pencil tip.
2. Ask students to predict if the spinner will land on a certain section. Have students spin their spinners and record the results. Compare the results to the predictions.
3. Create a new spinner with 3/4 of the spinner red and the rest blue. Ask, "What are the chances that the spinner will land on the red section?" Conduct the experiment and record the results.
4. Continue creating spinners, making predictions, and conducting experiments.

Group 2 ▢

Creating Spinners
1. Create a spinner. Have each student draw a circle in his math notebook and divide it into 2 equal sections. Color one section red and the other blue.
2. Ask students to use the new vocabulary words (*certain*, *likely*, *unlikely*, and *impossible*) to predict if the spinner will land on a red section. Spin the spinner 10 times and record the results.
3. Now, challenge students to create different spinners: one that makes it impossible to land on red, one that is equally likely to land on 3 different colors, and one that is certain to land on yellow.
4. After making the spinners, have students test them and record the results. Discuss the results as a group.

Group 3 △

Counter Probability
1. Use the colored counters from the mini-lesson. Ask, "How many counters are in the bag altogether? How many of those counters are blue? Red? If the counters were fractions, how could the number of blue counters be represented as a fraction? The red counters?"
2. Explain that the chances of choosing a particular counter can be explained more specifically than with the words *impossible*, *likely*, *unlikely*, and *certain*. Probability can also be expressed as a fraction, such as 9/10, and it is read as "9 out of 10."
3. Place a different combination of 10 colored counters in the bag. Have students determine the fraction that represents the probability of picking each color. Ask, "What fraction would represent a certain chance? What fraction would represent an impossible chance?"
4. Repeat with different combinations and total numbers of counters. Try providing fractional probabilities and having students put counters in a bag that match those probabilities.

Name_____

Draw a line to match each spinner with the most probable prediction.

1.

a. An equal chance of landing on any of the designs

2.

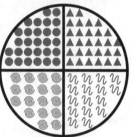

b. Impossible to land on a circle design

3.

c. A better chance of landing on a triangle than any other design

4.

d. Least likely to land on a heart design

5.

e. Equally likely to land on a circle design or a diamond design

6.

f. Least likely to land on a diamond design

Name_____

Follow each set of directions. Place a pencil at the center of the circle to hold a paper clip in place. Flick the paper clip so that it spins around the pencil tip.

1. Make a spinner that has an equally likely chance of landing on 4 different colors.

2. Spin the spinner 20 times and record your results.

3. Do the results show an equally likely chance of all 4 colors? Explain. _____

_____

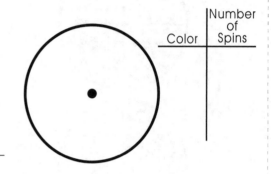

4. Make a spinner that has 3 different colors and is most likely to land on green.

5. Spin the spinner 20 times and record your results.

6. Do the results show a likely chance of green? Explain.

_____

_____

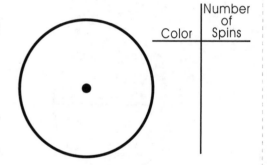

7. Make a spinner that has 2 different colors and is unlikely to land on blue.

8. Spin the spinner 20 times and record your results.

9. Do the results show an unlikely chance of blue? Explain. _____

_____

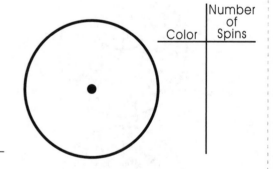

10. Make a spinner that has 6 different colors and is impossible to land on red.

11. Spin the spinner 20 times and record your results.

12. Do the results show an impossible chance of red? Explain. _____

_____

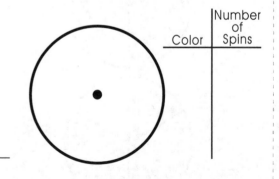

Name_____

Complete each sentence to explain the probability. Then, write the fraction to show the probability of the given outcome.

1. There are 3 blue counters and 9 red counters in a bag.

   There is a _____ out of _____ chance of choosing a blue counter.

   Fraction: _____

2. The letters in the word *arithmetic* are in a bag.

   There is a _____ out of _____ chance of choosing a vowel.

   Fraction: _____

3. There are 2 green sections, 3 yellow sections, and 1 purple section on a spinner.

   There is a _____ out of _____ chance of spinning yellow.

   Fraction: _____

4. You roll a normal 6-sided die.

   There is a _____ out of _____ chance of rolling an even number.

   Fraction: _____

5. Number tiles 1 to 12 are in a bag.

   There is a _____ out of _____ chance of choosing a multiple of 3.

   Fraction: _____

Answer Key

Page 7
1. tens 30; 2. ones 7; 3. hundreds 700; 4. thousands 6,000; 5. hundreds 500; 6. hundreds 400; 7. hundreds 200; 8. tens 40; 9. ones 1; 10. thousands 8,000; 11. 900 + 70 + 1; 12. 2,000 + 100 + 40 + 5; 13. 80 + 6; 14. 6,000 + 200 + 30; 15. 900 + 50 + 2; 16. 743; 17. 512; 18. 86; 19. 1,430; 20. 3,637

Page 8
1. thousands 5,000; 2. hundreds 100; 3. ones 4; 4. thousands 2,000; 5. hundreds 200; 6. tens 80; 7. tens 10; 8. ones 8; 9. thousands 2,000; 10. tens 0; 11. 5,000 + 800 + 90 + 7; 12. 2,000 + 300 + 8; 13. 5,000 + 200 + 30; 14. 7,000 + 800 + 70 + 6; 15. 3,000 + 800 + 70 + 6; 16. 3,458; 17. 4,681; 18. 3,523; 19. 2,564; 20. 4,735

Page 9
1. tens 0; 2. hundreds 100; 3. ones 4; 4. thousands 9,000; 5. ten thousands 90,000; 6. 30,000 + 8,000 + 800 + 10 + 2; 7. 30,000 + 2,000 + 600 + 80 + 7; 8. 50,000 + 9,000 + 4; 9. 30,000 + 8,000 + 900 + 10 + 2; 10. 40,000 + 40 + 5; 11. 34,753; 12. 63,471; 13. 35,284; 14. 50,027; 15. 67,274; 16. 55,345; 17. 97,432; 18. 940; 19. 67,000; 20. 85,400

Page 11
1. 20; 2. 80; 3. 40; 4. 10; 5. 40; 6. 90; 7. 50; 8. 40; 9. 100; 10. 60; 11. 200; 12. 900; 13. 800; 14. 600; 15. 100; 16. 700; 17. 300; 18. 800; 19. 600; 20. 900

Page 12
1. 200; 2. 800; 3. 900; 4. 200; 5. 200; 6. 600; 7. 400; 8. 500; 9. 400; 10. 400; 11. 2,000; 12. 9,000; 13. 5,000; 14. 6,000; 15. 8,000; 16. 2,000; 17. 6,000; 18. 4,000; 19. 7,000; 20. 10,000

Page 13
1. 20, tens; 2. 15,000, thousands; 3. 8,000, thousands; 4. 300, hundreds; 5. 70,000, ten thousands; 6. 73,980, tens; 7. 90, tens; 8. 40,000, ten thousands; 9. 600, hundreds; 10. 4,620, tens; 11. 70, tens; 12. 500, hundreds; 13. 10,000, thousands; 14. 600, tens; 15. 7,000, thousands; 16. 82,000, thousands; 17. 40, tens; 18. 3,000, hundreds; 19. 50,000, ten thousands; 20. 720, tens

Page 15
1. 90; 2. 81; 3. 73; 4. 60; 5. 82; 6. 70; 7. 75; 8. 77; 9. 57; 10. 83; 11. 74; 12. 80; 13. 95; 14. 99; 15. 90; 16. 85; 17. 47; 18. 81; 19. 67; 20. 40

Page 16
1. 561; 2. 811; 3. 953; 4. 740; 5. 242; 6. 700; 7. 815; 8. 568; 9. 820; 10. 832; 11. 5,382; 12. 9,600; 13. 9,507; 14. 9,019; 15. 6,510; 16. 5,219; 17. 8,144; 18. 9,665; 19. 8,029; 20. 8,961

Page 17
1. 7,443, Didn't regroup to the tens or the hundreds places; 2. 9,773, Didn't regroup to the hundreds place; 3. Correct; 4. 100,760, Didn't regroup to the tens or the ten thousands place; 5. 61,089, Didn't regroup to the thousands place; 6. Correct; 7. 50,092, Didn't regroup to the thousands or the ten thousands place; 8. 96,246, Didn't regroup to the hundreds or the thousands place; 9. Correct; 10. 61,990, Didn't regroup to the tens or the ten thousands place

Page 19
1. 26; 2. 11; 3. 65; 4. 8; 5. 8; 6. 17; 7. 11; 8. 55; 9. 19; 10. 4; 11. 33; 12. 12; 13. 14; 14. 3; 15. 46; 16. 12; 17. 11; 18. 30; 19. 46; 20. 38

Page 20
1. 12; 2. 68; 3. 29; 4. 45; 5. 24; 6. 377; 7. 376; 8. 532; 9. 286; 10. 450; 11. 4,600; 12. 5,958; 13. 1,757; 14. 1,976; 15. 8,591; 16. 579; 17. 3,578; 18. 3,505; 19. 1,916; 20. 579

Page 21
1. 200, 204; 2. 350, 359; 3. 700, 705; 4. 150, 155; 5. 3,000, 2,772; 6. 1,000, 1,150; 7. 1,000, 960; 8. 2,000, 2,273; 9. 19,000, 19,146; 10. 55,000, 55,957; 11. 25,000, 25,784; 12. 9,000, 9,106; 13. 49,950, 49,957; 14. 25,000, 25,556; 15. 50,000, 50,577

Page 23
Answers will vary.

Page 24
1. 1, 2, 5, 10; (1, 10), (2, 5); 2. 1, 13; (1, 13); 3. 1, 3, 5, 15; (1, 15), (3, 5); 4. 1, 2, 4, 8, 16; (1, 16), (2, 8), (4, 4); 5. 1, 2, 3, 6, 9, 18; (1, 18), (2, 9), (3, 6)

Page 25
1. Answers will vary but may include: 2, 3, 5, 7, 11, 13, 17, 19, 23, 29; 2. 4, 9, 16, 25, 36, 49, 64, 81, 100, 121; 3. Answers will vary but may include: 4, 6, 8, 9, 10, 12, 14, 15, 16, 18; 4. (1, 30), (2, 15), (3, 10), (5, 6); 5. 1 x 20, 2 x 10, 4 x 5; 6. 1 x 36, 2 x 18, 3 x 12, 4 x 9, 6 x 6; 7. 1 x 48, 2 x 24, 3 x 16, 4 x 12, 6 x 8; 8. 1 x 50, 2 x 25, 5 x 10; 9. A prime number is a number that only has itself and 1 as factors. Composite numbers are numbers with factors other than 1 and themselves. 10. Factors are numbers that can be multiplied with another number to get a product. Factor pairs are pairs of numbers that are multiplied together to get a product.

Page 27
1. 20, 10 + 10; 2. 60, 15 + 15 + 15 + 15; 3. 24, 12 + 12; 4. 42, 14 + 14 + 14; 5. 60, 10 + 10 + 10 + 10 + 10 + 10; 6. 33, 11 + 11 + 11; 7. 52, 13 + 13 + 13 + 13; 8. 0; 9. 80, 20 + 20 + 20 + 20; 10. 60, 12 + 12 + 12 + 12 + 12; 11. 50, 10 + 10 + 10 + 10 + 10; 12. 26, 13 + 13; 13. 14; 14. 22, 11 + 11; 15. 45, 15 + 15 + 15; 16. 54, 18 + 18 + 18

Page 28
1. 80; 2. 120; 3. 426; 4. 440; 5. 360; 6. 330; 7. 148; 8. 136; 9. 81; 10. 108; 11. 1,500; 12. 99; 13. 500; 14. 1,400; 15. 192; 16. 180

Page 29
1. 2,304; 2. 3,185; 3. 1,563; 4. 7,209; 5. 3,736; 6. 338; 7. 4,200; 8. 1,736; 9. 2,856; 10. 4,625; 11. 3,735; 12. 12,835; 13. 65,640; 14. 9,340; 15. 31,524; 16. 4,005

Page 31
1. 3; 2. 3; 3. 6; 4. 5; 5. 2; 6. 13; 7. 4; 8. 6; 9. 1; 10. 4; 11. 4; 12. 3; 13. 4; 14. 3; 15. 2; 16. 9

Page 32
1. 9, 9; 2. 6, 6; 3. 4, 4; 4. 9, 9; 5. 8, 8; 6. 9, 9; 7. 4, 4; 8. 4, 4; 9. 5, 5; 10. 4, 4; 11. 5, 5; 12. 9, 9; 13. 6, 6; 14. 5, 5; 15. 6, 6; 16. 9, 9

Page 33
1. Divide by 10; 2. Divide by 5, 6, 20;
3. Divide by 20, 8, 100; 4. Divide by
3, 8, 27; 5. Divide by 15, 2, 75;
6. Divide by 7, 12, 63; 7. Answers will
vary. 8. Answers will vary.

Page 35
1. 2/4 = 1/2; 2. 4/6 = 2/3; 3. 7/8;
4. 2/3; 5. 5/8; 6. 3/4; 7. 6/8 = 3/4;
8. 3/6 = 1/2; 9. 3/4; 10. 2/2 = 1

Page 36
1. 1/2 + 1/2 = 2/2 = 1; 2. 1/3 + 2/3 =
3/3 = 1; 3. 1/5 + 4/5 = 5/5 = 1; 4. 1/8
+ 7/8 = 8/8 = 1; 5. 1/6 + 5/6 = 6/6 = 1;
6. 2/4 + 2/4 = 4/4 = 1; 7. 3/8 + 5/8 =
8/8 = 1; 8. 2/5 + 3/5 = 5/5 = 1; 9. 3/10
+ 7/10 = 10/10 = 1; 10. 2/8 + 6/8 = 8/8 = 1

Page 37
1. 6/5 = 1 1/5; 2. 7/6 = 1 1/6; 3. 5/4 =
1 1/4; 4. 6/4 = 1 2/4 = 1 1/2; 5. 4/3 =
1 1/3; 6. 8/6 = 1 2/6 = 1 1/3; 7. 11/10
= 1 1/10; 8. 6/4 = 1 2/4 =1 1/2;
9. 15/10 = 1 5/10 = 1 1/2;
10. 9/5 = 1 4/5

Page 39
1. 7; 2. 5; 3. 4; 4. 4; 5. 12; 6. 1; 7. 3;
8. 6; 9. 8; 10. 9; 11. 4; 12. 9; 13. 2;
14. 10; 15. 12; 16. 0; 17. 14; 18. 3;
19. 3; 20. 2

Page 40
1. 8; 2. 9; 3. 5; 4. 25; 5. 6; 6. 45; 7. 3;
8. 42; 9. 10; 10. 5; 11. 60; 12. 20;
13. 40; 14. 25; 15. 367; 16. 70; 17. 34;
18. 50; 19. 10; 20. 3

Page 41
1. 80; 2. 150; 3. 700; 4. 45; 5. 455;
6. 130; 7. 600; 8. 5,800; 9. 12;
10. 2,000; 11. 640; 12. 65; 13. 200;
14. 500; 15. 3,000; 16. 8; 17. 4,000;
18. 0; 19. 5,000; 20. 3,000

Page 43
1. +; 2. +; 3. x; 4. –; 5. –; 6. x; 7. ÷;
8. x; 9. –; 10. ÷; 11. +; 12. –; 13. x;
14. +; 15. –; 16. ÷; 17. x; 18. +; 19. ÷;
20. + or –

Page 44
1. +, +; 2. ÷; 3. –, +; 4. x, +; 5. ÷; 6. –,
x; 7. ÷, +; 8. x; 9. –; 10. x, x; 11. –;
12. +, +, –; 13. x; 14. ÷; 15. x, ÷;
16. –; 17. ÷; 18. +; 19. –; 20. +

Page 45
1. x, +; 2. +, x; 3. +, x; 4. –, x; 5. ÷, x;
6. x, –; 7. ÷, –; 8. –, +, x; 9. x, –; 10. ÷;
11. +, –, x; 12. ÷; 13. –, ÷; 14. +, ÷, x;
15. x, x, +; 16. x; 17. +, x, +; 18. +, x;
19. +, x, –; 20. –, +, +

Page 47
1. 12 + 6 = 18 apples; 2. 6 x 3 = 18
wheels; 3. 18 – 6 = 12 cats; 4. 5 x 4 =
20 rocks; 5. 21 ÷ 3 = 7 grapes

Page 48
1. a; 2. c; 3. d; 4. b; 5. c

Page 49
Answers will vary.

Page 51
1. ○△▢○○△▢○
2. ▢○◇▢○◇
3. △▱▱△▱▱
4. ○◇○○○◇○○
5. ▭▭○○▭▭○
6. ▢△▢△
7. ◇○▢△◇○▢△
8. ○▭▢○○▭▢○
9. ▱○○◇▱○○◇
10. ○○▢○○▢

Page 52
1. e; 2. c; 3. h; 4. i; 5. d; 6. a; 7. f; 8. j;
9. b; 10. g

Page 53
1. 7 squares, 9 squares, 10th item has
19 squares, rule = add 2 squares;
2. 8 circles, 10 circles, 10th item has
20 circles, rule = add 4 circles;
3. hexagon, heptagon, 10th item has
12 sides, rule = add 1 side

Page 55
1. Add 10; 2. Subtract 5; 3. Add 9;
4. Add 7; 5. Subtract 3; 6. Add 2

Page 56
1. Subtract 10; 2. Add 15, 185, 395;
3. Multiply 6, 48, 66; 4. Add 25, 270,
950; 5. Times itself, 36, 64; 6. Add
150, 390, 450; 7. Answers will vary.
8. Answers will vary.

Page 57
1. Subtract 150, 650, 350; 2. Multiply
2, 136, 81; 3. Multiply 3, 225, 105;
4. Multiply 10 then add 2, 702;
5. Multiply 5 then add 1, 31, 41;
6. Divide 2, 500, 100; 7. Answers will
vary. 8. Answers will vary.

Page 59
1. 1.5 inches; 2. 3 inches;
3. 3.75 inches; 4. 1 inch; 5. 2 inches;
6. 3.75 inches; 7. 1 inch; 8. 3.5 inches;
9. 0.5 inch; 10. 2.5 inches

Page 60
Estimates will vary. 1. 1.5 inches;
2. 3 inches; 3. 3.25 inches; 4. 1 inch;
5. 2 inches; 6. 3.75 inches; 7. 1 inch;
8. 3.5 inches; 9. 0.5 inch; 10. 2.25
inches

Page 61
Answers will vary.

Page 63
1. 6, 10; 2. 20, 18; 3. 12, 14; 4. 12, 16;
5. 5, 12; 6. 8, 12; 7. 24, 22; 8. 32, 24

Page 64
Rectangles with a perimeter of 24: 1
x 11 (Area = 11), 2 x 10 (Area = 20),
3 x 9 (Area = 27), 4 x 8 (Area = 32),
5 x 7 (Area = 35), 6 x 6 (Area = 36);
Rectangles with a perimeter of 30: 1
x 14 (Area = 14), 2 x 13 (Area = 26),
3 x 12 (Area = 36), 4 x 11 (Area =
44), 5 x 10 (Area = 50), 6 x 9 (Area
= 54), 7 x 8 (Area = 56); 1. 15 square
centimeters, 16 centimeters; 2. 8
square inches, 12 inches; 3. 36 square
millimeters, 26 millimeters; 4. 49
square feet, 28 feet

Page 65
1. Area = 5, Perimeter = 10;
2. Area = 8, Perimeter = 14;
3. Area = 8, Perimeter = 14;
4. Area = 7, Perimeter = 16;
5. Area = 5, Perimeter = 11;
6. Area = 7, Perimeter = 16;
7. Area = 7, Perimeter = 14;
8. Area = 5, Perimeter = 12;
9. Area = 10, Perimeter = 14;
10. Area = 8, Perimeter = 8

Page 67
1. 6; 2. 24; 3. 45; 4. 20; 5. 60; 6. 24;
7. 90; 8. 56; 9. 32; 10. 210

Page 68
1. 36 cubic units; 2. 40 cubic units;
3. 48 cubic inches; 4. 84 cubic
centimeters; 5. 120 cubic yards; 6. 30
cubic meters; 7. 280 cubic inches;
8. 216 cubic millimeters; 9. 252 cubic
feet; 10. 216 cubic centimeters

Page 69
1. 2 x 6 x 3 = 36 cubic units; 2. 4 x 5
x 5 = 100 cubic units; 3. 6 x 1 x 4 =
24 cubic units; 4. 8 x 3 x 3 = 72 cubic
units; 5. Possible answer: 2 x 3 x 10 =
60 cubic units; 6. Possible answer:
1 x 15 x 3 = 45 cubic units;
7. Possible answer: 6 x 4 x 1 = 24
cubic units

Page 71
1. d; 2. g; 3. a; 4. h; 5. c; 6. f; 7. b;
8. i; 9. e

Page 72
1. rhombus; 2. pentagon; 3. trapezoid;
4. parallelogram; 5. octagon;
6. triangle; 7. Answers will vary.
8. Answers will vary. 9. Answers
will vary.

Page 73

Parallel Lines: trapezoid, rhombus, square, parallelogram, rectangle, hexagon, octagon

Right Angles: square, rectangle

Congruent Sides: equilateral triangle, rhombus, square (other possible entries: hexagon, octagon, pentagon)

Odd Number of Vertices: triangle, pentagon

Even Number of Sides: trapezoid, rhombus, square, parallelogram, rectangle, hexagon, octagon

Page 75

1. c; 2. b (and sometimes c); 3. c, d; 4. e; 5. b; 6. a

Page 76

Examples in real life will vary.
Cube: 6 faces, 12 edges, 8 vertices, dice; Rectangular Prism: 6 faces, 12 edges, 8 vertices, cereal box; Square Pyramid: 5 faces, 8 edges, 5 vertices, Egyptian pyramids; Sphere: 0 faces, 0 edges, 0 vertices, basketball; Cylinder: 2 faces, 0 edges, 0 vertices, soup can; Cone: 1 face, 0 edges, 0 vertices, funnel

Page 77

1. c; 2. f; 3. a; 4. e; 5. b; 6. d

Page 79

1. b; 2. a; 3. c; 4. b; 5. c; 6. a

Page 80

1. right and scalene; 2. obtuse and isosceles; 3. acute and equilateral; 4. right and scalene; 5. acute and isosceles; 6. obtuse and scalene; 7. right and isosceles; 8. acute and equilateral

Page 81

Answers will vary.

Page 83

1. 7 students; 2. 7 years old; 3. 8 years old; 4. 13 students; 5. 0 points; 6. 6 students; 7. 5 students; 8. 20 students; 9. 2 kids; 10. 14 kids; 11. 2 kids; 12. 2 books; 13. 2 students; 14. 4 students; 15. 5 students; 16. 15 students

Page 84

Answers will vary.

Page 85

Answers will vary.

Page 87

1. 7 students; 2. pizza; 3. grilled cheese; 4. 25 students; 5. 4 students; 6. swimming; 7. 9 students; 8. tennis

Page 88

1. 70; 2. 55; 3. 90 – 55 = 35; 4. Answers will vary. 5. 400; 6. 400; 7. 700 – 250 = 450; 8. Answers will vary.

Page 89

Answers will vary; sample answers given. 1. 50s; 2. No, numbers are too high for tallies to be practical. 3. No, data cannot be displayed along a number line. 4. Horizontal, because there is more space for longer bars; it is easier to compare long bars viewed horizontally. 5. 8; 6. Bar graph, because you can quickly and visually see data. 7. No, the data is not collected over time. 8. an eye, 1 eye = 2 kids

Page 91

1. c; 2. a; 3. b; 4. e; 5. f; 6. d

Page 92

Answers will vary.

Page 93

1. 3 out of 12, 3/12; 2. 4 out of 10, 4/10; 3. 3 out of 6, 3/6; 4. 3 out of 6, 3/6; 5. 4 out of 12, 4/12

96